ICE HOUSES OF IRAN

Where · How · Why

MAZDA PUBLISHERS

WITH GRANTS FROM: THE IRANIAN INSTITUTE FOR CULTURAL AND SOCIAL STUDIES, TEHRAN
VELUX FOUNDATION, COPENHAGEN – IRANICA INSTITUTE, IRVINE CALIFORNIA
BOARDROOM GORILLAS – A.K. JABBARI CHARITABLE TRUST

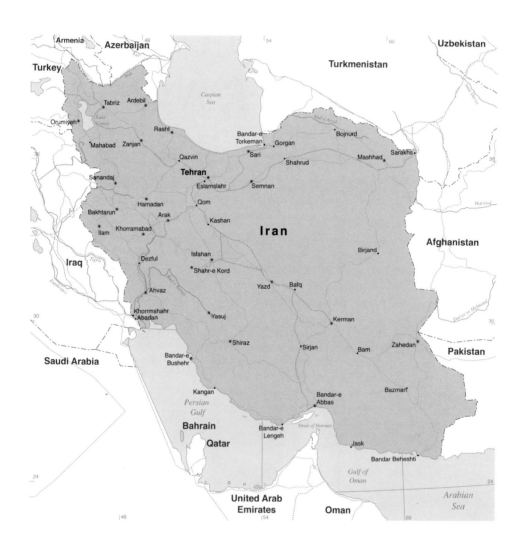

Bibliotheca Iranica

Archaeology, Art and Architecture Series, No. 2

Hemming Jorgensen

ICE HOUSES OF IRAN

Where · How · Why

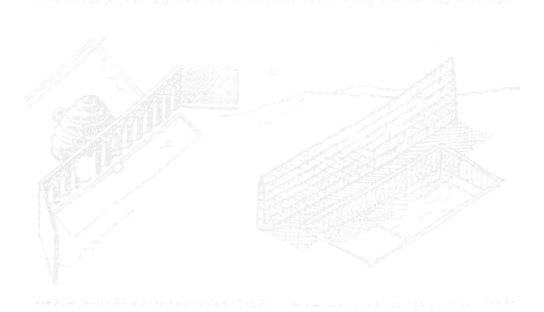

Mazda Publishers · Costa Mesa · California · 2012

Mazda Publishers, Inc.
Academic publishers since 1980
P.O. Box 2603
Costa Mesa, California 92628 U.S.A.
www.mazdapub.com
A. K. Jabbari, Publisher

Library of Congress Cataloging-in-Publication Data

Jorgensen, Hemming, 1939-
Ice Houses of Iran : Where, How, Why / by Hemming Jorgensen.
pages cm — (Bibliotheca Iranica. Archaeology, Art & Architecture ; No. 2)
Includes bibliographical references and index.

ISBN 13: 978-1-56859-269-5 (alk. paper)
ISBN 10: 1-56859-269-8
1. Icehouses—Iran. 2. Vernacular architecture—Iran. I. Title.
NA8350.J67 2013
725'.35—dc23
2012016877

Contents

Figures

Preface

The Iranian natural ice houses are an important part of the traditional desert architecture. However, the remaining elements and ruins of this unique type of vernacular building are facing a sorry fate after the last ones went out of use about 50 years ago.

The origins of the Iranian ice houses may be traced back to that of the qanat, the ingenious subterranean water supply tunnels, which were first observed in northwestern Iran almost 3000 years ago. However, only very limited textual, and no archaeological material exists concerning the traditional mud-brick ice houses of the Persian Plateau. That is the reason for writing this book, which is based on my research and ensuing doctoral dissertation entitled "Ice Houses of Iran – An Examination of the Evidence", University of Copenhagen, 2010.

On the basis of comprehensive field work, which included survey and registration of still identifiable ice house sites, my investigation endeavoured to answer the questions as to where, how and why the ice houses were built, operated and now largely forgotten. In the survey, I registered 129 ice house sites, of which the remnants of ice houses were found on only 104 of them. The Ice House List, Fig. 4.3, and the relevant location map, Fig. 4.4, are the most important documents, as they form the basis for – and the key to – the typology, analyses and conclusions derived from the findings of the project. Parts of the 500 page Ice House Catalogue that was appended to the dissertation, with all data, photographs and drawings obtained during the study, have been incorporated into this book. However, if a reader should wish details from the catalogue, such information can be requested via the web site www.hemmingjorgensen.com. Unless otherwise noted, all photographs and plans are by the author.

This study is the first comprehensive research dedicated to the traditional Iranian ice houses, and the study triples the number of previously registered examples in Central Iran. However, no ice house exists anymore in its original form and full extent. Unless a concerted effort is made in terms of restoration and preservation, the prognosis is not good for the majority of Iran's ice houses.

During my research I have received inspiration and help from many individuals. I wish to thank especially Professors Claus V. Pedersen and Peder Mortensen from the University of Copenhagen for their advice, and Professors Rémy Bourcharlat of France, Hassan Fazeli of Iran, and Alan Walmsley of Denmark for their appreciation and encouragement. Many Iranian friends, old and new, officials and private persons, high and low, have gone to great lengths to help me during the field work in Iran in the years 2007 to 2009. My sincere thanks go to all of them. Finally, I wish to thank the Iranian Institute for Social and Cultural Studies, which in October 2011 awarded me the esteemed Farabi International Award for my ice house research, and subsequently supported the publication of this book.

Hemming Jorgensen
Copenhagen, May 2012

1 | Introduction

Opposite page
YC·80 Alyan from distance

General remarks

The aim of this book is to present the results of a comprehensive field survey of the ice houses of the Iranian Central Plateau in the period 2007 to 2010. The book endeavors to answer the questions as to where, how and why the ice houses were built, operated and largely forgotten.

The *Oxford Universal Dictionary* defines an ice house as "a structure, often underground, and with non-conducting walls, in which ice was stored for use during the year" (1967: 949). In its simplest form an ice house compares with a storage clamp for potatoes or turnips, which is just a simple ditch or pit in which a stockpile of root crops are stored under protective layers of straw and earth for use during the winter. The Iranian ice houses were usually more sophisticated, as we shall see.

I saw my first Iranian ice house in 1966. My work as a civil engineer took me to Kerman in southeast Iran where a 20 meter tall mud brick dome outside town caught my attention. Local people told me that it was an old *yakhchâl*, or *yakhdân*, meaning an ice reservoir or ice pit. The Persian term *yakhchāl* is nowadays common throughout Iran as a designation for a refrigerator in a kitchen. But the word as originally used means "ice hollow" or "ice pit" (*yakh* means ice, and *chāl* means a hollow or a pit in the ground). This may suggest that the first Iranian ice storage facilities were simple earthen pits, in which solid ice was stored and covered with straw, rush and earth for protection and insulation against the heat and sunshine. The classical Greek writer Athenaeus noted that during his Indian campaign (327-326 BC) Alexander the Great "*dug 30 refrigerating pits which he filled with snow and covered with oak boughs. In this way.... snow will last for a long time*" (James and Thorpe 1994:322). Although the origin and chronology of ice pits in Iranshahr remain undocumented,

Athenaeus' account indicates that the technique of storing snow and ice in earthen pits was known in the region in the 4th century BCE. It is possible that Alexander's army may have learned about such ice storage pits when passing through northern Iran during the year 330 BC.

The term "ice house" (bīt šurīpi) was first found in texts from the Kingdom of Mari, on the Euphrates River, that date back to the 18th century BC. They read: "*Zimrilim who built the icehouse*", and "*when my lord ordered me to build an icehouse, I asked my lord for a master builder and they gave me the master builder PN, I had him build the ice house, and, having finished the icehouse, that man left for Mari.*" (CAD Vol. 17 III/1992: 348). The Mari ice houses were apparently used at the court to keep ice for cooling the King's wine; the ice blocks were brought in from the mountains in the region.

The ice houses of Mari were probably cellars within palaces, i.e. not the same type as the Iranian earthen pits, which with time were covered and protected by domes or cellar roofs, or provided with tall shading and sheltering walls on the south side and often at the east and west sides of the ice storage pit as well. The designation *yakhchāl* (ice pit) remains in use for such ice houses, and because of the sheltering superstructure the English term of "ice house" is suitable. The full Persian designation for an old ice house is *yakhchāl-e-ghadimi-va-sonnati* – an old, traditional ice house. In some regions, especially in Khorasan and Kerman Provinces, the Persian designation *yakhdān* (ice reservoir) often was - and still is - used for the old ice houses. The last traditional ice houses went out of use in the 1960s when mechanical, electrical- or kerosene-driven refrigeration became normal

Vent

Dome

Shade walls

Door to ice pit

Ice ponds

North

Fig. 1.2. Ice house at Abarqu, Iran. 2007[2]

across the country, including the Iranian Plateau, which had accommodated the majority of the natural ice houses due to its harsh climatic conditions, most especially the scorching heat of the summer.

An ice house would, naturally, store ice from winter for use in the summer. Ice houses have been well known in Europe for almost 400 years. The *Oxford Universal Dictionary* indicates the year 1687 as the earliest appearance of the term "Ice House" in the English language (1967:949). Beazley proposed that the English king, Charles II (1661-1700 AD), introduced the idea of keeping ice in an ice house on his return from exile (Beazley, E., and M. Harverson 1982: 50). However, Buxbaum notes that the first recorded ice house in London was built at Greenwich in 1619[1]. It was built as a brick well, 9 meters deep and 4.8 meters across, covered with a thatched timber structure (Buxbaum 2008:3). That ice houses were also used in Denmark, even before that time, is illustrated by Fig. 1.1, which shows the country mansion of the Danish king, Frederik II (1559-1588 AD), near Elsinore, with the thatched building in the garden presumed to be an ice house (Troels-Lund, T. 1915: 105).

Ice houses have existed in Iran for hundreds – probably thousands – of years. A typical, traditional ice house is shown on the photograph in Fig. 1.2, taken during an initial reconnaissance trip in February 2007. It is located at Abarqu, some 160 kilometers southeast of Yazd, in Central Iran.

This ice house consists of the following elements:

- Dome. An approximately 20 meter-high dome – or cone - made of mud and mud bricks, with steps to allow external access for maintenance and repair of the outer surface. The dome had been restored and repaired a few years earlier. Perfect mud brick work forms the inner shell of the dome.
- Doors at the west (visible), east and southeast sides of the lower dome wall at ground level.
- Vent at the top of the dome.
- Ice pit. A four meters deep ice storage pit under the dome, with walls and flat bottom of in-situ clay material.
- Ice Ponds. Remains of long, shallow basins, in which ice once was made of water from a channel system that is not anymore traceable.
- Shade Walls. Remains of three long, tall walls – running east-west - that once shaded the ice ponds from the south side. It can be noted that the wall to the left is built of mud bricks, while the two other walls are built up of layers of mud/straw mix.
- A sign at the north side informs: Ice house made of mud bricks. Perimeter of dome: 64 meters. Height; 22 meters.[3] Wall thickness; 3 meters. Depth of storage: 4 meters. Qadjar Period (1796 - 1925 AD) origin.

In terms of preservation, one notes with concern that the recently restored dome is already crumbling at the top; that no attempt has been made to preserve the shade walls, the ice-making ponds and the water supply system; and that buildings and power lines are getting dangerously close to the site of the historical monument. This is an alarming situation because this monument of utilitarian desert architecture may well decay further or even vanish in a few years time.

During my years of living and working in Iran between 1966 and 1978, I observed ice houses at several locations, in Kerman and Abarqu, also in Sirjan, and I heard of a former ice house in *Khiyâbân-*

e-yakhchâl (i.e. Ice House Street) in Gholhak, northern Tehran, where I once lived. Many years later, in 2006, I came to think of the magnificent structures I had seen on the Iranian Plateau in my young days and wanted to learn more about them. And while Iran is famous for its rich cultural heritage, and a vast literature has been produced over the ages within the fields of archeology, architecture, art and other cultural disciplines, very little has been written about ice houses. In fact, no comprehensive study of this important element of traditional Iranian vernacular architecture, or a consideration of its distribution across the Iranian landscape, has ever been written. My main motivating factor for the present study was to do something about this shortcoming, well knowing that a complete and comprehensive account of all the ice houses could probably never be attained.

Initial hypotheses

This project started out on the basis of a series of hypotheses and assumptions, some of which I tested preliminarily in an initial reconnaissance phase in order to ascertain whether an ice house survey would make sense:

· A comprehensive inventory of Iran's ice houses has never been made.
· A complete survey is probably impossible, but worth a try.
· Iran's ice houses had tall clay domes over an ice pit and large shade walls on the side as observed at Abarqu.
· Ice houses were organic inventions, built of local materials directly available, by local people, with no mechanical gear or support, and operated with renewable energy resources.
· The local materials used were mud and mud bricks, as is generally used for vernacular buildings near the deserts.
· Mud brick ice houses were mainly a rural phenomenon and typical for the Iranian Plateau.
· Ice houses were located near old settlements because they went out of use generations ago and there would consequently not be any ice houses at new residential areas.
· Ice houses were made to meet a need for cooling of drinks and food in the scorching hot summers and could be operated be-

cause of the availability of water, in combination with an arid continental climate that offered dry freezing nights for open-air ice production in winter.

· Due to the winter frost there would be no palm trees at ice house sites.
· Ice house development and use were linked to the development and use of the renowned subterranean irrigation water canals, i.e. the *qanât*, which brought sweet water from the mountains out into the plains near the large deserts.
· Ice houses have existed in Iran since c. 400 BC, or even earlier.
· Ice houses suggested luxury and were predominantly found in relatively well-off rural communities.

Already at the early stages of the project I noted for some ice house complexes the indications of an early co-operative association and for some others signs of local entrepreneurs, who had exploited a business opportunity. People I had met in early 2007 in Abarqu explained about the co-operative nature of the ice house operation that existed until 1960, and how it had been subordinated to the formalized trust that governed the essential business of *qanât* building and operation. Whereas the *qanât* venture was usually run like a corporation (a *vaqf*, see later), involving cash payments, *"the ice house venture was no vaqf because there was no money involved"*.[4]

State of research

The lack of any substantial and comprehensive research about Iranian ice houses, or even a basic typology, has been an important motivating factor for this project. There is, in fact, very little literature available on ice houses, and none pertaining to the existence of ice houses in Iran before the 17th century AD. In this chapter, I review the existent literature and the incomplete official Iranian registry of ice houses.

Michell has suggested that the manufacture of ice, and subsequent storage in large domed ice houses of mud brick, was a method possibly introduced into Iran by the Mongols, in the 13th century (1978: 206). However, there is strong circumstantial evidence for ice houses in Iran long before the 5th century BC, and for their

enhanced development and distribution after King Darius II at that time introduced tax incentives for the development of irrigation systems, of which ice houses are a derivative.

The popular use of ice and snow in Iran for the cooling of drinks and food was first reported by several European travelers in the 17th century AD (Beazley, E., and M. Harverson 1982: 49). In Thomas Herbert's description of Isfahan in 1628, he explained that "...*towards the outside of the city, large castle; unflanked but moated about; and several houses within, which guard the treasure, arms and ice there stored*"(1928: 127)[5]. Jean Chardin in his *Travels in Persia 1673-1677* described ice-making and the storing of ice in pits in the ground (1927: 239). Thévenot, who was in Isfahan about the same time as Chardin, also described ice-making (Lovell 1686: 96). Incidentally, the observations of these gentlemen took place at a time when the building of ice houses at castles and manors became fashionable in Europe, including England and Denmark, as mentioned above.

There is apparently only one reference in the 19th century to ice houses, when Jane Dieulafoy described domed ice houses in the vicinity of Tabriz, in northwestern Iranian, in the 1880s (Dieulafoy 1887: 55)[6].

There are more attestations of ice houses in the 20th century literature, but still very little information. In his last major work on Persian architecture, Arthur Upham Pope devoted only one paragraph to Persian domestic architecture, and one line to the ice houses: "...*and each town had immense water tanks and deep cisterns as well as carefully constructed ice-houses and reservoirs.*" (1965: 245). Another great personality within the inventorying of Iranian cultural heritage, André Godard, who came to Iran in 1928 at the request of the Iranian government to create an archaeological service, did not mention vernacular buildings at all in his *The Art of Iran* (1965). The same goes for Sylvia Matheson in her valued *Persia: An Archaeological Guide* (1972). The very comprehensive work, *The Traditional Crafts of Persia*, only mentions the existence of ice houses, but supplies valuable input for this project in terms of information on building crafts and materials (Wulff 1966). Volume 17, on caravansaries, of the comprehensive 20-volume Iranian architectural survey, *Ganjnâmeh* ("Treasure Chest"), includes photographs of the caravansaries at Dah Namak, near Garmsar, and at Meybod, near Yazd. Their respective ice houses are visible in the background of the photographs, but there is no mention of ice houses in the architectural survey reports. However, the "Lexicon" in the book contains an almost correct definition of an ice house (GN 2002: 11). In his book, *Persia, Bridge of Turquoise*, Roloff Beny illustrated the beauty of an Iranian ice house in a photograph entitled "*View from inside of a ruined ice house at the medieval town of Bam*" (1975: 40). However, more specifically useful information was provided by the French architect, Maxime Siroux, in the form of a surveyed cross section of a typical Iranian ice house, with two pages of accompanying text (1949: 131).

More informative sources include Beazley's *Living with the Desert* (Beazley, E., and M. Harverson 1982), which is a main inspiration for my own research. This important work deals with vernacular Iranian architecture, including structures such as water works, ice houses, wind catchers, watermills, windmills and pigeon towers, and the life associated with them (Beazley, E., and M. Harverson 1982). Bernard Hourcade also described an ice house at Kerman and one at Jaban in the Elburz Mountains, north of Tehran, and introduced the term "ice factories" (ateliers de glace) for these ice houses, because they each had an associated ice production facility (1994). This information corresponded to my own earlier observations at the ice houses in Kerman, Sirjan and Abarqu in the 1960s and 1970s. In addition, Porter and Thévenart, in *Palaces and Gardens of Persia*, devoted a section to "Cisterns and ice houses" and described a typical ice house like those just mentioned in some detail. They quoted Jane Dieulafoy, who 120 years earlier had observed near Tabriz "*a large number of ice houses in which the ice sold at the bazaar in summer is frozen and stored during the cooler months*" (Porter and Thévenart 2003: 33).

Three of the current travel guide books give indications of the situation of the still existing ice houses at Meybod/Yazd, Abarqu, Kerman and Malayer (Baker 2005; Loveday, H., B. Wannell, and C. Baumer 2005; and Burke 2004/2008). A number of other authors mention ice houses, their design and operation. However, they visited ice houses as tourists and misunderstood the operation of ice houses (e.g. Rutstein, H., and J. Kroll; Zanger). Articles about ice houses can be found on popular science internet sites (Wikipedia and alike), but most of the articles simply quote each other and the value of the information is dubious.

Two books in Farsi, largely inspired by the writings of Beazley and Wulff, were used during the recording and analysis of the field results to substantiate and confirm the findings of the project: *An Introduction to the Iranian Rural Architecture* (2006), donated to me by the author, Professor Akbar Zargar of Shahid Beheshti University Tehran at my visit in 2007, and *Climatic Analysis of the Traditional Iranian Buildings* (1994), by Vahid Ghobadian, bought in a Tehran book store in 2008. With the permission of Professor Zargar, it was possible for me to review and photograph a number of pages of hand-written reports on a) a student's field trip in search of ice houses between Kermân and Kâshân, and b) the restoration of the Arbab Taghi ice house in Tehran by the Municipality of Tehran.

A staff member of the Cultural Heritage Foundation in Kerman kindly supplied photocopies of drawings (with layout and section) of six of the ice houses in Kerman Province. A similar hospitality was experienced in Semnan, where pages from appraisal reports for four ice houses could be photographed by me.

The main local personal contacts and sources are listed below:

- Mr. Mehdi H (b.1948), whose father (d. 1981) was a co-owner of an Abarqu ice house.
- His cousin, Mr. Hamid M, a schoolteacher of Abarqu.
- Mrs. Shahla F (b.ca.1949), whose grandfather (d. 1960) built and was the owner of the Firouzabad village and associated ice house, near Damghan.
- Mr. Mostafa S (b. ca.1962), a high school teacher of Damghan.
- The Iranian Ambassador in Copenhagen (2008, Mr. Morshidzadeh), and fellow travelers on planes and buses in the years 2007-2009.
- A large number of friends, names unknown, who proved very helpful on the way as guides and drivers/assistants.

Ice houses in the National Registry

It was as late as in the 1970s that the Iranian authorities began to be interested in ice houses, and official registration took place in the provinces of Isfahan, Tehran, South Khorasan and Kerman. At a visit to the Iranian Archaeological Research Center in Tehran during the first field trip in 2007, I received a "complete" list of Iranian ice houses registered by the Cultural Heritage Organization (*Mirâs Farhangi*). When I received the list of ice houses, I was stunned at first, because to establish such a list was my primary objective. To my "relief" I had discovered already some ice houses that were not on the list. I received further confirmation that the list was far from complete when in the summer of 2008 I managed to obtain the official *Iranian Artifacts Registered in the List of National Monuments* (Pazooki and Shadmehr 2004). This National Register contains 13,300 artifacts. Of this number, 6,648 artifacts concern not only vernacular structures, but also mausoleums, gardens, dams, bridges, passion play buildings, monasteries, churches, houses, towers of silence, mansions, palaces, gates, observatories, hot springs, schools, and laundries. It also contains 56 ice houses spread over Iran, while the list from the Research Center had only been an extract, or rather a first page of two, with 31 entries. So, my project was still justified. The Research Center was at the time of my first visit in the process of issuing a book on Iranian ice houses and the work seems still underway.

As just noted, the National Registry (NR) indicates that the number of registered ice houses as of 2004 is 56; however, this does not necessarily mean – as we shall see – that all of these still exist as monuments or ruins. Some have disappeared completely. When split up into provinces (*ostân*), the distribution of NR registered ice houses is as follows:

West Azerbaijan	3	Kerman	9
Isfahan	2	Mazanderan	2
Tehran	3	Markazi (Central)	I
Razavi Khorasan	II	Hamadan	I
South Khorasan	3	Yazd	5
Semnan	I6		

Of the 56 ice houses in the National Register, 47 are located on the fringe of the large central deserts – Dasht-e-Kavir and Dasht-e-Lut – of the Central Plateau of Iran, or in the highlands – with several local deserts – between the central deserts and the Zagros Mountains, stretching from the Esfahân to the Sirjân/Kermân areas. This area corresponds to what was subsequently defined as the Project Area at the outset of the project. Fig. 1.3 shows Iran's provinces with the respective numbers of registered ice houses. A total of nine of these are located outside the Project Area.[7]

The Project Area includes the provinces of Semnan, Isfahan, Yazd, and Kerman, largely in their entirety, as well as the parts of the provinces of Tehran, Qom, Markazi and Khorasan near large deserts.

The outline of the Project Area is a large polygon – or rather a triangular-shape band - enveloping the areas around the towns of Tehran, Saveh, Qom, Kashan, Isfahan, Sirjan, Kerman, and Bam in the west and south flanks, and the towns of Tehran, Garmsar, Semnan, Shahrud, Sabzevar, Nishabur, Khaf and Birjand in the north and east flanks. The Project Area covers around 250,000 km^2, about 15% of the total area of Iran.

Research objectives

The scarcity of data available before the inception of this project and the above challenging hypotheses led to the following main research questions for the project:

(a) How many Iranian ice houses have survived, bearing in mind that they have gone out of use and were built of perishable mud materials? Considering the vast spaces involved, does an inventorying survey make sense?
(b) What is their distribution? Is there a pattern in their distribution relative to topography and other environmental factors, such as soils, water and climate?
(c) What do the ice houses and their remains look like? Is there a variation in types from the examples I saw forty years ago in Kerman, Sirjan and Abarqu?
(d) What factors contributed to their construction and operation?
(e) What was their function in their respective localities?
(f) Can their origins and history be traced?
(g) What is the status nowadays regarding the preservation of ice houses?

The first stage in addressing these issues would be the comprehensive survey to locate still existing ice houses, and – to the extent possible - register those that have disappeared. The next stages would include investigations of the physical and social circumstances in which the ice houses were built and used.

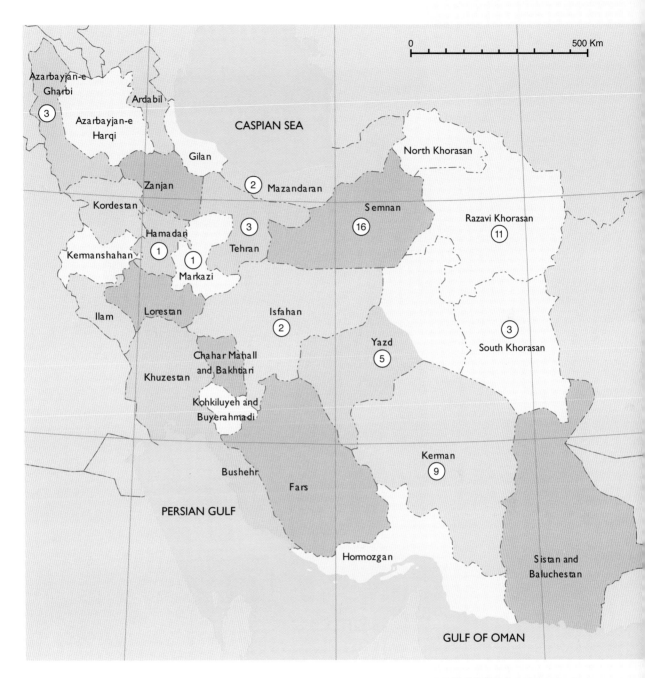

Fig. 1.3. Number of registered ice houses in Iran's provinces

2 | Ice houses Background

Opposite page
YC·125 Amrani fortress

Vernacular architecture

Vernacular language is that spoken by the people; vernacular building is that built by the people. Architecture without drawings might be another way of describing it (Beazley, E., and M. Harverson 1982: 11).

Ice houses, cisterns and water mills combine two skills in which the Iranians excel. First, the design and execution of domes and vaults in mud-brick, which result in beautiful buildings, often constructed for mundane purposes. Secondly, the Persian imagination and ingenuity, which is unrivalled in making the best use of water in a hostile desert environment. In this the Iranian contribution to the world's technology is probably unique (Beazley 1977: 89).

Until 40-50 years ago a huge legacy of fascinating and beautiful vernacular buildings – not only ice houses - still existed on the Iranian Plateau. The list of Iranian vernacular architecture is very long: water cisterns, wind towers, bazaars, dwellings, hunting lodges, bath houses, water-cooled rooms and cellars, windmills, watermills, lodging houses, fortresses, pigeon towers and, of course, ice houses. These structures represented the combination of creative building and structures adapted to the climate. Most of them occurred in villages, but some were found on a larger scale in and around the towns. Vernacular architecture as design is timeless. Yet, the sad fact is that since then many of these beautiful buildings have crumbled and disappeared completely. In the first instance, many mud-built dwellings and villages were abandoned because – despite their indisputable thermal properties – it was no longer fashionable to live in old-style buildings considered synonymous with lack of development, and often with poverty. A "normal" building, made of stone or baked bricks in a temperate climate, will survive for many years, even as a ruin. But the Iranian vernacular buildings are chiefly made of sun-dried mud bricks and mud-paste. Any such building will quickly deteriorate without constant maintenance. And the fierce climate of the Iranian Plateau, and the occasional earthquake, accelerates the decay process. The worst enemy, however, are modern buildings in primitive fired bricks, concrete, steel and glass, which gradually supplant the traditional buildings and increase the need for fossil fuel-driven cooling or heating.

Scattered settlements have existed for thousands of years near the foot of the mountains and bordering the large deserts of the inner plateau of Iran. The settlements were very similar in building style because climate and topography imposed the same conditions for survival on each of these isolated communities. This is the background for the development over time of a particular vernacular building style - desert architecture - around the central deserts of Iran. Thick mud walls and domed roofs were standard building elements along the desert edge where stone and timber were scarce raw materials. It is, therefore, possible to observe certain common features among the dwellings and amenities of communities as widely apart as Khaf and Birjand in the east, Sabzevar, Shahrud, Semnan and Damghan in the north, as well as Kashan, Nain, Yazd, Kerman and Sirjan in the south and south-east, within the horseshoe-shaped area bordered by the Elburz and Zagros mountains (Beazley, E., and M. Harverson 1982: 2). This is why one can, as demonstrated by the present study, observe ice houses of similar style in Semnan, in the Yazd area, and in Kerman and Sirjan, a thousand kilometres further south.

Social context

In tandem with the architectural legacy, there is also a striking continuity of tradition over a period of over a thousand years; the present social structure still includes some features inherited from earlier periods going back as far as 350 BC (Ghirshman 1965: 289ff). For instance, the traditional rural structure, before land reform, was determined by the *boneh*, a collective production unit (Farshad, A., and J.A. Zinck 1997: 2), in which landlords should provide seed corn, water and safety. This prevailing pattern, with share-crop peasants, was broken in 1962-63 by the land reform of the so-called White Revolution.[8] This change happened to approximately coincide with the demise of the traditional ice house system.

Besides having suitable building designs, Middle Eastern residents have made use of a series of passive cooling systems from antiquity up to the present. Soflaee and Shokouhian (2005: 715) list some natural passive cooling systems of traditional architecture: *bâdgir* (windcatcher, tower or stack), *showadân* (underground room), *shabestân* (basement room), *sardâb* (outside or indoor space with flowing water), *sabat* (roofed passage), *khishkân* (hut with mats to be splashed with water), *hayât* (courtyard), *havâkesh* (air vent). They are all related to natural ventilation and reduction of exposure area towards the hot atmospheric air and the sun.

The ice house was also a natural element of accommodating to an arid environment. The usual Persian term for an ice house is *yakhchâl* or in Eastern Iran sometimes *yakhdân*, meaning ice chamber or ice reservoir. In some contexts the word *barfdân*, i.e. snow chamber or reservoir, is heard. The storage of compacted snow is often practiced in mountainous regions or on the plain when no ice is available in the village vicinity. *Barfdân* falls outside the scope of the present study as they were usually small and/or placed inside the house walls for household use. The term *yakhchâl* is nowadays also used for a standard kitchen refrigerator. The ice houses under investigation in this project have therefore been termed "*yakhchâl qadimi va sonnati*" (old traditional refrigerator) in conversations with Iranian source contacts.

Chronology

As mentioned at the beginning of the book, the oldest references to ice houses in the Near East date to the Middle Bronze Age from the Kingdom of Mari (see p. 2). Probably based on the same sources, James and Thorpe likewise report that around 1700 BC Zimri-Lim, ruler of Mari, boasted in one of his inscriptions of having constructed near his capital a "*bit shuripim, which never before any king had built on the Euphrates*" (1994: 322). This approximate date is confirmed by a cuneiform tablet from around 2000 BC that tells of the ice house of an Assyrian governor, who used ice to chill his wine in summer (Roaf in EVA 1997/I: 465). However, the ice houses in the palaces of King Zimrilim and the Assyrian governor were probably cellars within the palaces, i.e. not of the same type as the Iranian free-standing domed mud brick structures, which covered an earthen pit.

Opposite page
Fig. 2.1. Assyrian village with high
domed roofs on Neo-Assyrian relief
(Larsen 1997: 189)

The Greco-Roman world probably borrowed the concept of construction of the ice houses from the east, either in the form of simple earthen pits or sheltered reservoirs as built in Iran. Unfortunately no documentation linking the ice house concepts of the two worlds could be found.

Other references to ice houses seem to describe types different from the ones of this study. From China archaeological confirmation comes from the Ch'in Dynasty (221-207 BC): The capital built at Hsienyang by the first emperor, Shih Huang Ti, included a luxury version of the simple ice pit. Made of huge ceramic rings, it was sunk forty-three feet into the ground (James, P., and N. Thorpe 1994: 322). The oldest remains of an ice house in China – indeed in the world, James claims – were discovered in 1976-77 during excavations of the palace at Yongcheng, an ancient capital in Shesi Province. Built in the seventh century BC, it had a design different from that made for the first emperor: a shallow pit was framed by double wooden boards with an insulation made of rice husks between them (1994: 322). Access was by a ramp, which went down to sluice gates. A drain was built into the ramp to draw off water from thawing ice. Beazley also suggests that ice houses were known as early as the 8th century BC in China and that they were probably small thatched buildings (Beazley, E., and M. Harverson 1982: 50), which incidentally corresponds to the design observed in Denmark (see Fig. 1.1 on page 2 of the Introduction). During the Tang Dynasty of China (618-906 AD), the literary work known as the *Shih King* ("Food Canons") speaks of the rituals surrounding the maintenance of ice houses as a time-honored custom (James, P., and N. Thorpe 1994: 322).

Much later there are reports that the Ottoman palace of Topkapi, in Istanbul, had an ice house near the kitchen (Hildenbrand 1994: 454). In Europe, ice houses became fashionable in the highest circles of society during the 17th century AD. As noted earlier, the first British ice house was built in Greenwich in 1619 (EVA 1997 I: 465).

Only from the 17th century AD do we find descriptions of observations of ice houses in Iran by various travellers (Fryer 1912, Chardin 1927, Herbert 1928, Dieulafoy 1887). Not even such a keen observer as Marco Polo, who travelled through a bitterly cold Kerman province in the winter of 1271 and observed a qanat some 100 kilometers north of the town, ever mentioned ice houses.[9]

Although the earliest documented ice houses in Iran date back only to the 17th century AD, it seems reasonable to suggest, consider-

Fig. 2.2. A cluster of domed Syrian village houses still in use (c. 1995, Puett 2005: 101)

ing the evidence from the Near East dating to as early as the Middle Bronze Age, that some form of ice storage was also prevalent in Iran from a much earlier date. However, the absence of evidence, both textual and archaeological, for the presence of ice houses in Iran - or for their origins and development there - in pre-Islamic times has been confirmed by personal communication with leading scholars within the fields of iranology, archaeology and architecture (Professor Ehsan Yarshater of Columbia University, Professor Pierre Briant of College de France, and Professor Susan Roaf of Herriot-Watt University).

The origin of the Iranian desert ice houses can therefore not be documented, however buildings with dome-shaped roofs were known in the Near East already in prehistoric times at Chogha Mish (6800 to 3000 BC) in the Susiana Plain in southwestern Iran[10] and at Tell Arpachiyah (6100 to 5400 BC) in Northern Iraq (Leick 1988: 202). The oldest illustration of high domed buildings was found on reliefs in the palace of the Neo-Assyrian King, Sennacherib (704-681 BC), in Nineveh (Larsen 1997: 188-190; Puett 2005: 102-104), cf. Fig. 2.1. In these reliefs, village houses with high domed roofs are shown in the Assyrian countryside.

This type of domed village architecture can still be found in many locations in Syria, in hot and arid landscapes like the Idleb and Aleppo steppeland (Larsen 1997: 190), cf. Fig. 2.2. The Syrian domed buildings were – and are still today on a limited scale – used for dwellings, stables, granaries, storage, and ovens (Puett 2005: 101; Grube 1978: 180; Nippa 1991: 34).

In Iran, domed buildings of a size and shape similar to the Syrian ones were apparently used only for utilitarian purposes, e.g. water reservoirs and ice houses. But these domed buildings served a similar purpose of combating the extreme heat of a near-desert region. Persians have always had a passion, almost addiction, for iced drinks and iced food (Farshad, A., and J.A. Zinck 1997: 2). During the ages, drinking water was cooled in porous ceramic jugs or jute bags turned cold by evaporation. But nothing beat ice for drinks; ice was almost a necessity for life; and necessity is the mother of invention (Dickson 1924: 9). The demand for ice was the driving factor, but a combination of other factors supported the invention of ice houses. The qanats ran throughout the year, and water was in surplus during winter. The surplus water would freeze in ponds, basins, and lakes, and it was easy to dig holes for storing the ice and later to cover it. The efficiency of the storage would increase dramatically by building a dome over the ice storage pit, and the whole exercise could be done by local people without outside help.

I suggest, then, that the Iranian ice house was invented as a natural derivation of the qanats, which in Iran came into use at the beginning of the 1st millennium BC (Goblot 1979: 67). The development of qanat systems gained speed when about 400 BC King Darius II granted tax concessions for the building of irrigation systems, including *qanât* (Briant 2001: 389). Perhaps Alexander's ice storage facilities in India, mentioned above, might have been copied from examples he came across on his way through Persia, where Darius had expanded the *qanât* system by his tax relief less than 100 years earlier. It may follow from these suggestions that ice houses in the form constructed by Alexander in India already could have been in use in Persia in the 4th century BC.

The unfortunate situation remains that no archaeological evidence or literature on ice houses before the 17th century AD, when the oldest of the ice houses of the present survey were built, exists. Maintenance and occasional major repairs have also made the original shapes and materials hard to identify. Still, though lack of evidence will remain a problem, there is plenty of scope for improving the difficult historical jig-saw puzzle (Skibo, J.M., and M.B. Schiffer 2008: 2). Perhaps the technique used by Alexander the Great in India might indicate that today's ice houses could already have existed in a simpler but similar form in Persia already in the 4th century; this very interesting supposition deserves further investigation.

Ownership and role

Unfortunately, no ice houses were situated at the few rural communities where there have been studies that have explored the material, social, and cultural dimensions of human settlement and architecture (for instance, Horne 1994; Fazeli, Salami and Young 2009). However, in general, qanats, water tanks and ice houses could be owned by either a vaqf, a landlord, or a cooperative.

From the Semnan *Mirâs Farhangi* appraisal reports (1999, in Persian, barely readable) the following remarks on ownership and operation are available:

- The ice house Shah Djugh Kuchek (YC·71)[11] was public; all people could use it. Ownership was unknown.
- Shah Djugh Bozorg ice house (YC·72) had a small house for the workers to use in the cold winter nights. Ownership was unknown. It took usually six weeks to fill an ice house in the Semnan area. The ice blocks were crushed and water poured over to obtain a solid mass of ice in the storage.
- Bostam ice house (YC·103) was used for storing foodstuff and drinks for public use. The last manager (*Yakhchâli*) was Mohamad Taqi Saidi, who financed the ice production and sold the ice in the summer time. The ice house was vaqf-owned. There is a similar situation for Saadabad (YC·90).
- The Sarkheh ice house (YC·68) was a donation to the public by the deceased businessman, Hadj Abdollah Azizi.
- In the Semnan area, one owner was called "*Halva'i*" because besides ice he sold "*Halva*", a Persian sweet consisting of flour, sugar and oil.
- The *Mirâs Farhangi* documents about the Semnan water buildings (1999) explain that the rural ice houses could be owned by a vaqf, by landlords, cooperatives and local businessmen (halvâ'i).

Hourcade reported that the majority of ice houses in the Kerman area belonged to traders, who until the beginning of the 1960s sold the ice directly to people or in the bazaar. But a large number of those in villages were built as a charitable institution (*vaqf?*) for the villagers. The ice house at Abbasabad (YC·24) was built by Haji Agha Ali, a great landowner, who had possessions near Rafsanjan and in the villages near Qasemabad and Ismailabad. The ice was given free of charge to the peasants who worked on all his lands; the day-workers enjoyed the same privilege. Surplus ice was sold to the other villagers. And similar conditions prevailed at the ice house of Kabutar Khan (YC·25) (Hourcade 1994: 94).

Ghobadian argued that the domed ice houses in the villages belonged to a vaqf or a confectioner (halva'i), which is only partly true. He quotes a Mr. Ernest Houster (?): "*There are many ice houses, some of them private and even the poor people could use them for drinks. Shops with lemonade and fruit used ice. It was possible to buy ice from stalls in the bazaar and directly from the ice houses. Also blocks of ice were sold from street vendors with donkeys*" (Ghobadian 1998: 329).

From her travels in Iran in the 1880s, Jane Dieulafoy reports on her observations near Tabriz of ice houses made of unbaked brick domes: "*Though the cost of ice is very reasonable, each yakhchâl earns its owner between one hundred and two hundred tomans*" (Porter and Thévenart 2003: 34) (a toman at the time was worth the equivalent of $1.70).

My own travels provided the following information:

· On my question about ownership of Abarqu I (YC·37), Hamid M, one of my contacts there, presumed that there once had been a "Malek", an owner, but he was not sure.
· Shahla F, of Damghan, relates that her grandfather and his cousin owned the entire village of Firouzabad, including the ice house (YC·75), which he built in the 1930s. The ice house was part of his estate and delivered ice to his own household, but also to people in the village.
· Mehdi H, of Abarqu, relates that his father was part of a co-operative of farmers that owned and operated the ice house Abarqu II (YV·38). The cooperative was a no-cash organization subordinated to the vaqf that owned and operated the qanat.
· The high school teacher, Mostafa S, of Damghan, explains: "*After having sold the ice, and having covered their expenses, the owners shared the revenue among themselves.*"

Hourcade claimed that it was often the case that the ice houses, or a share of the production, belonged to vaqfs (trusts) created by present or former owners, as was the case for qanats and the water tanks (Hourcade 1994: 95). The qanats and their output were usually vaqf-owned, with the local mullah as the chairman. On my question to Mehdi H whether the Abarqu II ice house was a vaqf system the answer was, *"No, because there was no profit involved."*

The institution of the vaqf is basically Islamic, but its legal aspects had been incorporated into the civil legislation of Iran long before the Islamic Revolution in 1979. A *vaqf* can be constituted as a charitable interest, or for private purposes. As Mehdi H told me, a vaqf offered protection against the government, theft, fraud and greed; anyone who broke the rules of the vaqf would be punished by God (i.e. would burn in hell). Mehdi H also explained that in the old days – before the Islamic Revolution - mullahs in the villages would consider themselves predestined to become chairmen of the *vaqf* that owned qanats and possibly ice houses. After the Islamic revolution, all vaqfs became state-owned and controlled by a particular ministry. Imam Reza (Mashad) had been a huge *vaqf*, and many people benefited from it; however, now that the trust is simply government property, people appear to have lost pleasure and initiative.

Generally, in the villages there was a clear distinction between the "haves" and the "have-nots". The "haves" were primarily the landlords, who, before the "White Revolution", owned the majority of land in the villages, and in many cases entire villages. The rest of the population consisted of the share-crop peasants, the day workers, and their families. It may be concluded that the ice houses were built primarily to supply ice in the summer to their owners – the "haves" – but that there were provisions for supplying fixed rations to the poor, the "have-nots", as indicated by many citations in recent literature, and in the following:

- *"So common is the use of ice that the poorest are enabled to have it, and even the bowls of water for gratuitous drinking in the street are cooled by it"* (Beazley, E., and M. Harverson 1982:50).
- *"In the villages the ice was handed out on a daily agreed and weighed basis to owners and workers and the rest of the day's ration given to the poor".* (Local contact Mehdi H)
- *In Rafsanjan: "The ice was given free of charge to the peasants who worked on all his lands. The day-workers enjoyed the same privilege. Same at Kabutar Khan"* (Hourcade 1994: 94).
- *The Iranian method was so developed that even poor people could have ice for drinks* (Ghobadian 1998: 329).

In summary, the ice houses that were built in some of the near-desert villages in the Project Area were primarily owned and operated by either private landlords, vaqfs or cooperatives. While the poor part of the population in landlord-owned villages was dependant on these individuals, they usually received ice as a generous gesture and were better off than people in other villages. Due to their role as public utilities with a religious input, the vaqfs would endeavor to be fair to all, which included ice for the poor. In the case of cooperative ownership, ice was probably given as remuneration for work, but also as a gesture to the poor. The feeling of community around the ice house – regardless of ownership - was confirmed by the big village parties held when the ice house was full and sealed in the late winter and when the ice seal was broken around mid-summer.

The large town ice houses were industrial enterprises, where the ice was split up into groups of different quality and sold at the gate, delivered to small butchers, dairies, restaurants, or sold in the streets. I remember that in the 1970s it was still possible to have ice blocks delivered at our house in Tehran.

3 | The Investigation

Opposite page
YC·39 Abarqu III

General environmental conditions of the Project Area

Ice houses form part of the Iranian vernacular architecture which comprises the near-desert buildings of the Iranian Plateau. The building of ice houses was driven by local demand, caused mainly by the intense heat during summer. But the ice houses could only be feasible if the following factors were favorable: (a) the environment, including topography and climate, (b) the soils for both agricultural and building purposes, and of course (c) the hydrology and availability of water. These three main factors were decisive for the agricultural potential on the desert perimeter. The dwellings, the water reservoirs, the irrigation systems and, most particularly, the ice houses would never have come into existence without a suitable combination of the environmental conditions and man's ability to exploit them.

The greater part of Iran is situated on the plateau, which falls away in the centre and east to the great central salt desert - an arid, uninhabited, trackless space (Lambton 1953: 1). This vast desert, covering many thousands of square kilometers at elevations between 550 and 1500 meters above sea level, was in the past crossed only by a few tracks and shunned even by the nomads. It is one of the driest and, in summer, one of the hottest places on the earth's surface (Beazley, E., and M. Harverson 1982: 1). Yet folk have come to terms with conditions on the edges of this inhospitable place, discovering millennia ago how to exploit the available water resources and how to develop a simple building style notable for its effective response to the climate and for its harmony with the surroundings (Ibid). In fact, most of Iran's great cities have developed in this fringe environment, along with thousands of smaller settlements.

It is the raised rim of the central desert that constitutes the Project Area. Towns like Nishabur, Damghan, Saveh, Qom and Kashan developed on the routes connecting the principal cities. And scattered along the base of the surrounding mountains are the villages, a particular part of whose local architecture constitutes the subject of this book. It appears that the villages around the large deserts are very similar because climate and topography imposed the same conditions for survival on all of these isolated communities (Beazley, E., and M. Harverson1982: 2).

In geological terms, the Iranian Plateau is a late formation. As late as the Mesozoic era (c. 60 million years ago), most of the land was covered by a large sea, called the Sea of Tetis (Ghirshman 1954: 21). When this sea drained, its remnants became the Caspian and the Black Seas. The lasting effect of the Tetis has been the persistence of salt deserts in Iran and the existence of at least one highly condensed salt lake, Urmia, in Western Iran. The Caspian, the largest lake in the world, also has a high salt content (Dewan M.L., and J. Famouri 1964: 26; http://forum.hyeclub.com).

The Iranian Plateau today is a land surrounded by high mountains. Two important mountain ranges, each with peaks over 5000 meters high, stretch from the northwestern corner of the Plateau to the east and to the south. The eastern branch, Elburz, boasts the highest peak, Mount Demavand, at 5671 meters above sea level, situated only 70 kilometers northeast of the capital, Tehran. The Elburz range creates a high barrier south of the Caspian Sea, making serious impacts on the climate of the Plateau. While lush forests and pastures abound along the southern banks of the Caspian and give it a mild, humid climate, the Elburz prevents the passing of the rain-rich clouds on to the Central Plateau, causing very low rainfall, and consequently creating a dry and mostly warm climate south of the mountains. The second mountain range, the Zagros, stretches from the northwest to the south and diverts to the east just north of the Persian Gulf. It does not have as much influence on the climate of the Plateau as the Elburz Mountains (CHIr, Vol. 1, 1968: 91).

Topography

The Project Area is situated in and below the piedmont zone of the mountain ranges surrounding the central deserts, Dasht-e-Lut and Kavir-e-Lut. Figure 3.1 illustrates a cross section of the desert fringe with its four environmental zones. The upland zone consists

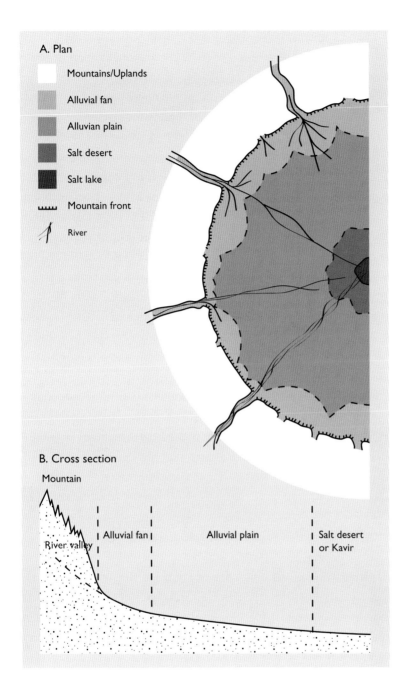

A. Plan

- Mountains/Uplands
- Alluvial fan
- Alluvian plain
- Salt desert
- Salt lake
- Mountain front
- River

B. Cross section

Mountain

River valley

Alluvial fan

Alluvial plain

Salt desert or Kavir

Fig. 3.1. Desert fringe schematic (Beaumont et al. 1988: 29)

of mountains, which include the Zagros range in the west, the El-burz range in the north, and the highlands of East Iran. The three other morphological zones are all depositional in nature. The alluvial fan zone is situated at the boundary of the upland zone and is characterized by ground surface slopes from 15 degrees down to about 3 degrees. The surface of the alluvial fan is relatively flat. The Project Area is located within the "Alluvial Fan" and "Alluvial Plain" zones.

Coarse sediments, both angular and rounded, make up most of the alluvial fan zone. Deposition of sediment is brought about by both fluvial (river deposits) and mudflow activity. Usually, mudflows from the high areas only penetrate as far as the upper parts of the alluvial fan zone, while river flows often continue into the two lower zones as well (Beaumont, P., G.H. Blake, and J.M. Wagstaff 1988: 30).

The alluvial plain and the salt desert zones are continuations of the alluvial fan zone. The alluvial plain displays lower ground surface angles than the fans, and in many parts of the Middle East, including the perimeter area of the Iranian Plateau, it forms the major morphological zone. The plain is mainly formed by the depositional action of running water spreading out from streams in the mountains, and the soil composition becomes more fine-grained with increasing distance from the mouth of the mountain streams. In some areas the finer material is removed by the wind, leaving a stone or desert pavement behind. The salt lake, or salt desert zone, only occurs in basins with no drainage outlets, as is the case in Central Iran. Soils in this zone are normally fine grained, of silt or clay size, with the coarser material having been deposited during its passage at higher water speeds over the alluvial fan and plain zones. The project survey indicated that the village ice house sites were usually located on the alluvial plains, on the desert rim, where the soils were found to be clayey, with varying content of silt (loam), fine sand and sometimes gravel (Ibid).

Climate

The climate of central Iran is one of extremes. The summer temperatures match those of the Persian Gulf and even surpass them. Winters are bitterly cold and bring snow in the mountains and sometimes in the desert too. In mid-winter the temperature in the central desert can range from -5C to +40 degrees C in the space of the six morning hours, which has an important bearing on the ice house project. The aridity of the land is enhanced by the regular strong winds usually coming from the north-east (Beazley, E., and M. Harverson 1982: 5).

Generally speaking, Iran has four climatic zones: (A) The southern shores of the Caspian Sea, with a temperate, subtropical climate, (B) The Northern shores of the Persian Gulf and the Sea of Oman, with a hot and humid climate, (C) The Mountain and High Plateau regions, including the Zagros and Elburz ranges, with a cold climate, and (D)

	Latitude N	Longitude E	Elev. M	No. Days Min. >21 C	No. Days Max. >30 C	No. Days Min. <-4 C	No. Days Min. <0 C	No. Days Prc. >5mm
Abadeh	31 11	52 40	2030	4	106	37	90	8
Abarkuh/Abarqu	30 56	53 23	1485	20	157	43	91	5
Anar	30 53	55 15	1409	28	157	20	62	5
Ardekan/Yazd	32 19	54 01	1104	60	171	29	71	5
Ardestan	33 23	52 23	1252	103	142	7	31	7
Bafgh	31 36	55 26	991	77	189	5	30	4
Bam	29 06	58 21	1067	145	191	1	9	4
Biarjamand	36 03	55 50	1106	57	122	31	85	9
Birjand	32 52	59 12	1491	24	142	31	76	13
Doushan Tappeh	35 42	51 20	1209	98	126	8	39	19
Isfahan	32 37	51 40	1550	34	128	24	73	9
Ferdous	34 01	58 10	1293	41	140	14	58	10
Garmsar	35 12	52 16	825	75	154	13	52	9
Ghaen/Qaen	33 43	59 10	1432	5	104	42	94	13
Ghazvin/Qazvin	36 15	50 03	1279	7	113	38	90	22
Ghom/Qom	34 42	50 51	877	56	158	19	64	10
Gonabad	34 21	58 41	1056	52	140	11	49	10
Kabootarabad	32 31	51 51	1545	6	129	42	96	7
Karaj	35 55	50 54	1313	21	108	24	65	17
Kashan	33 59	51 27	982	87	160	8	43	9
Kashmar	35 12	58 28	1110	69	134	7	36	15
Kerman	30 15	56 58	1754	11	137	43	88	10
Khoor	32 56	58 26	1117	104	163	9	37	7
Mashhad	36 16	59 38	999	12	106	36	89	18
Naein	32 51	53 05	1549	36	125	18	63	8
Natanz	33 32	51 54	1685	68	91	17	58	13
Neyshabur	36 16	58 46	1213	4	113	31	90	17
Rafsanjan	30 25	55 54	1581	50	147	8	41	7
Sabzevar	36 12	57 43	978	67	145	20	59	13
Saveh	35 03	50 20	1108	91	139	7	37	14
Semnan	35 35	53 33	1131	97	137	9	45	10
Shahr Babak	30 06	55 08	1834	13	125	45	92	11
Shahreza	31 59	51 50	1845	9	111	39	86	10
Shahroud	36 25	54 57	1345	28	94	26	81	10
Shargh Isfahan	32 40	51 52	1543	7	133	58	109	7
Shomale Tehran	35 47	51 37	1548	60	97	16	56	27
Sirjan	29 28	55 41	1739	36	139	17	61	7
Tehran Mehrabad	35 41	51 19	1191	83	126	12	48	16
Torbate Heydarieh	35 16	59 13	1451	18	107	40	96	19
Yazd	31 54	54 17	1237	81	161	13	51	4
Average			1331	49	134	23	65	11

The Central Plateau region, with a hot and dry climate (Ghobadian 1998: 13-18). The latter region includes the Project Area.

Meteorological data for the 40 stations located in or close to the Project Area – shown in Fig. 3.2 – have been obtained from the web site of the Iran Meteorological Organization (www.irimet.net). The site contains data up to the year 2005 for 154 recording stations

Fig. 3.2. Climatological data for the Project Area (www.irimet.net)

countrywide. The oldest of the stations have been operative since the 1950s, and a few only since 1995.

The geographical co-ordinates and elevations of the recording stations are shown, along with the annual numbers of days with (a) the minimum daily temperature of more than 21 degrees, (b) a maximum temperature over 30, (c) temperature under -4 Celsius, (d) sub-zero Celsius temperatures, as well as the number of days with (e) more than 5 millimeters of precipitation. For the forty weather stations in the Project Area the average altitude is 1331 meters above sea level, while the average altitude of the surveyed ice houses is 1222 meters, as we shall see later. Due to the differences in altitudes and locations between the weather stations and the ice houses, the meteorological data can only be considered as broadly applicable for the ice house sites.

The climate numbers have been extracted from a vast mass of data, and are intended to give some characteristic figures for the understanding of the conditions of the Project Area:

(i) The numbers of days during which the temperature is more than 21 degrees around the clock, i.e. the number of really hot nights, is on average for the Project Area 49 days. The warmest spot, the southeastern town of Bam, has 145 hot nights a year.[12]

(ii) The number of days during which the temperature rises above 30 degrees centigrade, i.e. the number of really hot days, is on average for the Project Area 134 days. The maximum of hot days per year (190) is reached at the towns of Bam and Bafq, situated some 200 kilometers southeast and northwest of Kerman, respectively.

Other above-average hot spots are Ardekan, Yazd, Kashan, Qom, Anar, Abarqu, Garmsar, Rafsanjan, Sabzevar, Birjand, Sirjan, Semnan and Kerman. As I shall demonstrate, all these locations are home to the majority of Iran's ice houses.

In terms of frost days, the average number per year of days with frost is 65 within the Project Area. And the number of days with a temperature of less than -4 degrees is on average 23, i.e. the potential for open air ice-making in winter is considerable in the Project Area. As a general indication, Hourcade (1994: 89) states that ice for ice house use can be produced when the annual number of frost days

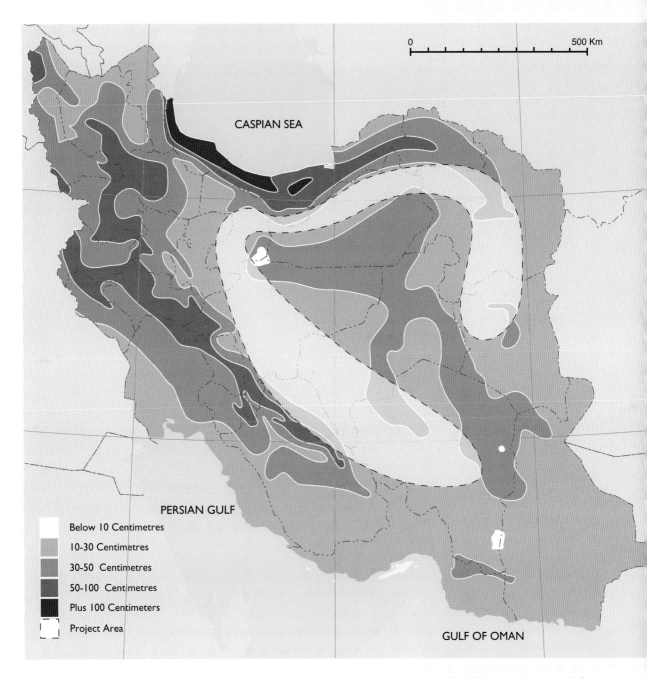

CASPIAN SEA

PERSIAN GULF

Below 10 Centimetres

10-30 Centimetres

30-50 Centimetres

50-100 Centimetres

Plus 100 Centimeters

Project Area

GULF OF OMAN

0   500 Km

Fig. 3.3. Precipitation map with Project
Area (after Elr 1989: I/33)

is at least 20. However, this indicated number of 20 days appears
to be on the low side, as my analyses will show. At the low end of
the scale, the town of Bam has only 9 frost days per year on average,
i.e. the potential for in-situ ice-making is low. Incidentally, Bam is
a large oasis town with thousands of date palms, which can sustain
temperatures down to about the freezing point. At a temperature
of minus five degrees they will lose their leaves (Nicolaisen 1978).

This indicates that the weather station is situated at a location that is more exposed than the oasis proper, which could well have a milder micro-climate inside the garden walls. All other weather station locations in the Project Area display an annual number of frost days of 30 or more, and a better potential for in-situ open air ice-making consequently exists. Some of the coldest spots, compared with the average of 65/23 days per year[13], are West Isfahan (109/58 days), Torbateh Heydarieh - 200 kilometers south of Mashad - (96/40), Qaen – 400 km south of Mashad – (94/42), Abarqu (91/43), Kerman (88/43), and Shahrud (81/26). The majority of the coldest sites are situated in the eastern part of Iran.

There are large temperature differences between sun and shade.[14] And, the diurnal temperature variation can be over 40 degrees. The summer temperatures during the day are around 40-50 degrees centigrade and at night within the range of 15-25 degrees. Long-wave radiation causes rapid loss of heat from the land surface during summer nights (surface temperature can fall from 70 to 15 degrees or below) (Givoni 1976: 342).

Of course, fresh water is also necessary for ice-making. Rain is scarce, as can be seen from Fig. 3.3, on which the Project Area has been superimposed on the Precipitation Map of Iran (EIr 1989: I/33). It can be seen that, with the exception of a small area around Nishabur in the east, and at Tehran and Kerman, the entire Project Area displays an annual precipitation of less than 200 millimeters, and a long stretch between Qom and Kerman – including the towns of Nain, Yazd, Abarqu and Anar in the hot center of Iran - even less than 100 millimeters. In the entire Project Area, ice house operation can only be possible if fresh water is provided by other means, i.e. either surface streams, pump wells or underground water supply channels (qanats) - or if the ice houses can be supplied with solid (pre-fabricated) ice from nearby mountain heights.

The rain falls during winter, if at all in a particular year, and then usually in heavy showers. The Cambridge History of Iran (CHIr 1968 Vol.1: 246) gives the following values of Mean Annual Rainfall (in millimetres):

Bam	76 mm	Isfahan	126 mm
Kerman	203 mm	Qom	144 mm
Shahrud	135 mm	Tabas	91 mm
Tehran	223 mm	Yazd	67 mm

For comparison, the annual rainfall at Rasht on the Caspian Sea is 1353 mm, and in Denmark on average 450 mm.

In the table in Fig. 3.2 with meteorological data, I have included the number of days with a precipitation amount of over 5 millimetres, as this number would roughly indicate how many times a year the mud brick buildings at a particular location would be subject to heavy rain showers, which would damage the clay plastered surfaces. For Bam, for instance, the Cambridge source gives an annual rainfall of 76 millimetres while the statistics indicate 4 days per year with a precipitation over 5 millimetres. This indicates that heavy showers are infrequent – maximum 4 – while the remainder of the annual rain falls as a drizzle, which adds up to the order of 50 mm per year. The situation at Yazd – at 67 mm of precipitation per year and 4 days with heavy rain – is similar to that of Bam. However, at Kerman, Shahrud and Qom– 203, 135 and 144 mm per year, respectively, and 10 days with heavy rain in all three locations - the rain erosion danger is greater. Within the Project Area the places with the highest number of rain days are in the Tehran area (Tehran, Doushan Tappeh and the old airport of Mehrabad) and at Nishabur where clay structures are exposed to 16 to 27 days of potentially dangerous rain showers.

Hydrology

Water is the key to all settlements on the Iranian Plateau. Without water there is no way of cultivating the fine-grained low quality soils, which otherwise display severe limitations for agriculture due to water deficit and salinity (Dewan M.L., and J. Famouri 1964: 17). Irrigation in the Iranian Plateau has been traditionally dependant on qanats, gently-sloping subterranean conduits which tap a water-bearing zone at higher elevations, usually in the piedmont zone of the adjacent mountains[15]. The qanat water tunnels enable the supply of fresh water to the majority of villages and towns within the Project Area.

The word *qanât* stems from Arabic (qanât (sg.), qanavât (pl.), ref. Persian-Danish Dictionary); sometimes the old Persian words kâriz or kâhriz are used, meaning a subterranean channel (DSDE 1999 Vol.15: 582 and Vol.10: 336).

The exact place and origin of the qanats is not completely clear. Goblot reported that cuneiform sources record that the Assyrian King Sargon II (722-705 BC), during his campaign in the area north of Lake Urmia in northwestern Iran, observed that agriculture prospered due to irrigation despite the lack of rivers (Goblot 1979: 67)[16]. Goblot suggested that qanats had developed in the early first millenium BC from the drainage galleries of the flint mines in the neighboring Urartu region (Ibid). The Assyrians adopted the qanat system during the reign of Sennacherib (705 -681 BC) at the end of the eighth century (Ibid). Qanats were being utilized by the time of the Achaemenid Empire (6th – 4th centuries BC), and the Persians introduced the technique into Egypt after they conquered it in 525 BC (James, P., and N. Thorpe 1994: 416). Besides spreading to Egypt, the use of qanats also spread eastward to Afghanistan (CHIr 1967: I/433).

The use of qanats in the Achaemid Empire was described by the Greek historian Polybius (ca. 200-118 BC), who was never in Iran and obviously must have used secondary sources to describe events that took place some three hundred years earlier. At any rate, Pierre Briant claims that the existence of qanats was confirmed at the time of Polybius, i.e. the 2nd century BC (2001: 18). Briant deals extensively with Polybius (his Vol. X.28) and expresses some doubt about the interpretation of the original Greek text. However, there seemed to be general agreement at a seminar in Paris presided over by Pierre Briant in 2001[17] that qanats must have existed in the Achaemenid era and were the basis of the power of the Achaemenids (Briant 2001: 18). Briant quotes Polybius for a "trustworthy tradition" that the Persian kings, when they were masters of Asia, gave to people who made new irrigation works the right to exploit the concerned land for five generations (Briant 2001: 18 and 38). This is the first steps of an agricultural policy by the ruling powers (Ibid). So, while the origin of qanats is uncertain, it appears confirmed that they existed during Achaemid times.

Boucharlat confirms the uncertainty about the time of the first qanats (in Briant 2001: 158), and Christensen bluntly states that "I am not aware of a single case where qanats have been dated back to pre-historical times with any reasonable degree of certainty on the sole basis of archaeological criteria" (1993: 129). On the basis of my investigations for the present project I must, with much regret, say the same thing about the ice houses of Iran. I assume, however, that the qanat technique spread from north-western Iran, where incidentally the annual precipitation is relatively high, i.e. 200-800 mm/year, into the Plateau, and particularly its fringes, where the annual precipitation is much less, under 200 mm/year (refer Fig. 3.3 on page 33).

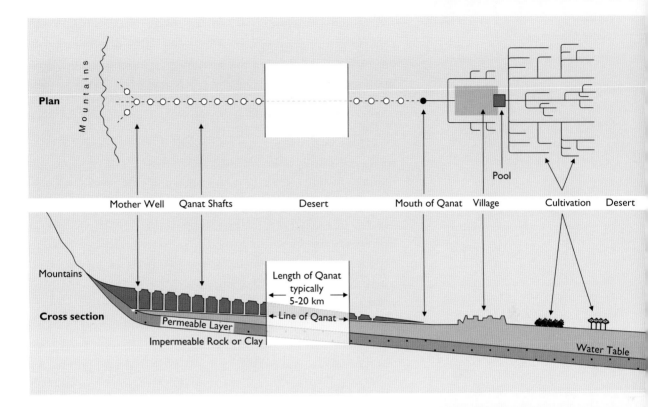

Plan

Mountains

Mother Well   Qanat Shafts   Desert   Mouth of Qanat   Village   Cultivation   Desert

Pool

Mountains

Cross section

Length of Qanat
typically
5-20 km
Line of Qanat

Permeable Layer
Impermeable Rock or Clay

Water Table

Fig. 3.4. Alluvial fan with qanat
(after Beazley, E., and M. Harverson
1982: 35)

The qanat water tunnels enable the water supply to reach and to irrigate lands situated at long distances from the mountains. Qanats carry water from areas of availability to areas of need (Tapper, R., and K. McLachlan 2003: 7). And, as noted above, the use of qanats probably began in Iran more than 2500 years ago, and from here spread eastward to Afghanistan and westward to Egypt (CHIr 1967: I/433). The qânat construction principles are shown in Figure 3.4.

The process of the construction of a qanat is begun by a "Water-Diviner" (*Muqanni-bâshi*), who, based on his observations and experience, finds an area near the mountains with signs (vegetation, dampness) of a large underground water-bearing stratum. Trial wells are subsequently dug to test the level and possible flow rate of the ground water. The successful well becomes the mother well which can be up to 100 meters deep, but usually much less, i.e. of the order of 15 to 30 meters. A line of vertical guide shafts is then dug at 100 to 300 meter intervals to give the line and depth of the future tunnel to the point where, with a minimum slope (about one meter in a thousand), it emerges on to the terrain surface. This future outlet point will become the qanat mouth and the starting point for a village or an orchard. The qanat diggers then commence their work (starting from downhill to avoid flooding during work) of digging a tunnel to the mother well(s). The diggers bring up the excavated soil through shafts at about 50 meter intervals. These shafts serve also as ventilation and access shafts. From an aerial view the qanat and its shafts appear like a line of mole hills, see Fig. 8.4 on page 205 of this book.[18]

Once completed, a qanat would consist of an underground water tunnel, usually unlined, with enough slope for the water to run from the mother well to the mouth, but at so slow a speed that erosion of the conduit is avoided, or kept to a minimum.[19] Because qanats rely on a gravity feed rather than pumping or other mechanical delivery systems, they reduce the rate of reservoir depletion during periods of slow replenishment (Strauss 2005). At the mouth of the qanat there would be a pool from which the villagers would fetch water for the households, and from which an elaborate system of channels would convey water to the gardens and the fields, based on an agreed set of rules for the distribution quantities and periods (Beazley, E., and M. Harverson 1982: 38). Also, a possible ice house, usually situated near the cultivated area, would be supplied from the qanat in the winter months when the water demand for irrigation would be at a minimum.[20] Along the open channels were often lines of trees for shade and protection. The qanats were owned by landlords or co-operatives, but most often by a "vaqf", as noted already a religious trust to protect and operate a community asset, separately from the land ownership (Lambton 1953: 220). Very elaborate rules were set up within a qanat vaqf to administer the distribution of water (Ibid; Beazley, E., and M. Harverson 1982: 39)

It is impossible to over-emphasise the importance of water and its traditional values to the Iranians, who for almost three thousand years have led a settled life in places which would have remained uninhabited elsewhere (Beazley, E., and M. Harverson 1982:30). Already in Achaemenid times (500 BC) this skill was an essential part of living: "*In the Avesta, the sacred book of the old Persians, irrigation was a good deed in the eyes of Ahura-Mazda… (and) the Achaemenid kings granted exemption from land-tax for five generations to all who made land cultivable by irrigation*" (Wulff 1966:245).[21]

According to its nature, a qanat runs uninterruptedly over the year, although with seasonal variations. But there is reduced demand for irrigation during the winter months, so it seems a natural idea to stem up the abundant water in shallow basins during the

winter and to let it freeze into ice blocks for later use, if it can be stored. The idea of storing ice blocks in a cool place led to the use of underground ice storage pits and chambers, in which the ice could be kept, without melting, into the scorching hot summers. This is the basic concept of an ice house, which in Iran combined the optimum use of local building materials with a better management of the resources in the form of water and ice. Indeed, the qanats are an outstanding invention. First, they are indigenous in all senses: the type of survey, construction, operation and maintenance, together with the supply of equipment and personnel - all can be accomplished with local and mainly rural resources. Secondly, there is no foreign dependency requirement in either initial construction or maintenance (Tapper, R., and K. McLachlan 2003: 7). Incidentally, the same can be said about the Persian ice houses.

The number of qanats has fluctuated over time. In 1950 the Irrigation Agency estimated that there were 32-40,000 still in operation throughout the country (Tapper, R., and K. McLachlan 2003: 8). In 1968 the number of qanats in Iran was of the order of 22,000, comprising more than 280,000 kilometres of underground channels (Wulff 1968: 94). After the Islamic revolution, when there was some government emphasis on preserving indigenous irrigation and farming structures, there were thought to be as many as 40,000 qanats in use (Tapper, R., and K. McLachlan 2003: 8). Nowadays, many qanats have been replaced by deep water wells with pumps, and the water management of the plains is in peril due to the uncontrolled exploitation of water resources by pumping over the last fifty years. The availability of diesel motor pumps in many areas has led to overwatering, with subsequent increased evaporation and salinization of the fields, sinking ground water levels and drying out of qanats. During my 20,000 kilometres of travel during the past three years, I noticed less than ten active qanats, and I saw only one team of qanat-diggers at work with their wind-lass (i.e. winch), at Shahr-e-Babak in February 2008. Ultimately, water has become scarce, making it difficult to cultivate new areas. 50 years ago there were 30 to 50 qanats in Abarqu in Yazd Province; in 2007 only 3 or 4 were still active. My contact Mehdi H explained to me that in 1950 the ground water table at Abarqu was 30 meters below the surface; in 2007 it had sunk to more than 200 meters beneath ground level. In addition, Boisen explains that in the 1930s there had been 60 qanats supplying the city of Tehran, of which the most famous was the "English Qanat", which brought water from the Elburz piedmont in the north of the city to the English legation downtown (1946:124). On my visits to Tehran in 2007 and 2008, great problems of flooding was experienced at the Old Shemiran Road, where the excavation works for a new metro line had hit an active qanat from the Elburz Mountains.

Methodology

The ice house project is highly empirical. The core activity of the project was to carry out an as comprehensive as possible inventory of Iranian ice houses on the fringe of the large deserts of the Iranian Plateau. This alone is a major contribution to the study of ice houses in Iran. In addition, the analyses of typology, construction, function, use, history, and current status move the knowledge about these structures far beyond the state of research as determined in Chapter 1. The field work included a total of six expeditions, with a total of 40 field days, 12 days with meetings with local contacts, and some 8 days with inter-city travels by bus or airplane. A total of 23,000 kilometers were travelled in Iran, of which 20,000 kilometers were in rented cars.

The first steps in expanding the inventory of ice houses in Iran included the following:

(a) The study of available literature and other material in order to obtain an idea of possible locations and criteria for the selection of such sites;
(b) Meetings with the cultural heritage authorities in Tehran and in the provinces to obtain concrete leads for the search in the field;
(c) A field search using the first indications as aids to expanding the survey. The equipment for the field work was comprised of a road map, a GPS location/altitude finder, a compass and altimeter as back-up, binoculars, a 10 mega-pixel digital camera, a meter tape and a folding ruler. I used local taxies for transport and explained to the drivers the purpose of the exercise so that they could assist in the ice house search. Obviously, the quality of the drivers as assistants varied immensely. If a visit was not possible or a search not successful, there was usually not another chance later due to the huge distances involved.

The results of the very first days of the survey indicated that there were more ice house types than exemplified by the "prototype" at Abarqu (Fig. 1.2), and that ice houses were not only located at desert villages but also at towns and caravansaries and forts. In addition, it became clear that not all ice houses had ice-making plants, as observed at Abarqu; a large number were simple ice storage facilities without a trace of an associated ice-making plant.

These facts necessitated the following steps:

· The introduction of a coding system in order to control the survey results and to enable the later development of a typology for the ice houses;
· An extension of the study of the literature to include background information about the environment, topography, geology and soil conditions, hydrology and climate.

Concurrently with the course of the field work the following studies were undertaken:

· Processing of the data collected; digitalization of maps and ice house coordinates.
· Analyses, evaluations and assessments relative to ice house registration, typology, operating methods, environmental and community context.
· Review and evaluation of the ice house situation today and the preservation aspects.
· Drafting work, writing, composing, proofreading and printing.

Transliterations of Persian (Farsi) words follow the rules of Vahman and Pedersen (1998), with one exception: The final h in many Persian words is maintained in this book. A minimum of diacritical marks is used: One only. The Alef, i.e. the long, dark "a", is transcribed as â and only when a Persian word's pronunciation is desired. In all other cases diacritical marks are omitted. The international reader will not be helped by their use, and the Iranian reader will hopefully understand.

The chronology in this book is based on the scheme in *Iran. A Chronological History*. (Alizadeh et al., 2002)

Limitations and problems

An attempt to obtain official Iranian recognition of and support for the project was only partly successful. An official request for accreditation in early 2008 from the Danish Embassy in Tehran to the Iranian authorities via the Iranian Foreign Ministry ended up at the Iranian Embassy in Copenhagen. An Iranian Embassy official kindly approached me, but could in the end not provide any official or practical support. On the positive side it could be noted that my trips and surveys were never obstructed in any way, and the reception at informal visits to various public offices around the country was always very forthcoming. My knowledge of the Persian language was an advantage and at the same time a limitation. The advantage was that I was able to travel alone and communicate with the local people; the drawback was that my Persian was not so accomplished as to allow full understanding of particular names of villages and sites. Some of the transcriptions of location names may therefore be incorrect or deficient, for which I ask for understanding.

It was an obvious limitation for the project that one man alone tried to cover an area of the order 250,000 km^2. However, it was attempted to minimize this drawback by focusing on areas where the existence of ice houses was indicated by leads obtained either from the literature or from local contacts. There were also other considerations – and combinations of them, based on the original hypotheses – which helped to focus the search:

- As ice houses went out of use 50-60 years ago, the search could focus on the areas around older settlements;
- Ice houses with an ice-making plant would be found only in areas with abundant sweet water;
- Rural ice houses would be found usually only at well-off village communities, due to their air of luxury;
- As palm trees cannot be sustained in frosty conditions, ice houses with an ice plant would not be found near palm groves;
- Ice houses were built with mud brick and mud plaster, i.e. suitable soils should prevail, not only as building material but also for agriculture;
- Ice houses would not be found in areas with temperate climate or where chilled water streams would bring cooling in summer, but only in regions with hot, dry, arid climate.

- Ice house operation would require a minimum number of freezing nights in winter, or the existence of a nearby mountainous area from which ice could be collected.

The use of a hand-held GPS apparatus delivered the North/East coordinates with an estimated accuracy of less than 5 meters. A few GPS measurements could not be made, either due to the proximity of a site to a military installation or due to momentary technical problems. The elevations were less exact as they were calculated by means of satellite triangulation; their accuracy is estimated at +/- 25 meters. The back-up altimeter, based on barometric pressure recording, was not used except for general checks, due to the constant need for altitude calibration, which could not be done during day-long missions due the lack of firm benchmarks.

Field notes were prepared for all sites visited. No real geodetic surveys were made at the sites. Only rough measurements were taken and the horizontal numbers checked and complemented by measurements on Google Earth satellite imagery, which was available for more than half of the sites. These horizontal measurements were used as the basis in calculating heights of domes and walls, chiefly in conjunction with an analysis of the more than 1,000 photographs taken on the sites.[22]

An Ice House Catalogue – which constituted an integral part of my original 2010 dissertation - was prepared on the basis of the field notes and photographs. It included drawings – with plan and cross sections – for a number of ice houses in the project area. The drawings are of varying accuracy, due to the source quality and the ensuing reproduction on the basis of photocopies and photographs. However, they are of great value for understanding the ice houses of Iran, and as a basis for further studies of the subject.

The drawings are based on three sources:

- photocopies of old photocopies of old drawings from the *Mirâs Farhangi* office at Kerman;
- photographs taken by me of drawings in *Mirâs Farhangi* appraisal reports at Semnan;
- photographs taken by me of drawings on the walls of the Water Museum in Yazd and the local archaeological museum at the Robat Karim Caravansary south of Tehran.

It should be noted that the dimensions of ice pits especially, as logged in the Catalogue, are encumbered with great uncertainties. Most ice pits visited during the survey were either filled up with garbage or soil, and some were locked up, so that their dimensions had to be guessed or assessed in broad outline. Thus, the ensuing analyses and statistics render only rough quantitative trends.

Ice houses are a disappearing phenomenon. No ice house has been preserved in the complete shape it once had when it was in operation. The ice-making facilities (ponds for ice-making, shading walls, and water supply channels), especially, have almost all disappeared. This has created a certain amount of uncertainty with regard to the correct classification of domed ice houses, i.e. whether they had an ice-making plant or not. Local sources in the areas of Garmsar and Nishabur reported that ice-making in many cases took place in open fields – without shading walls – so that the absence of shading walls does not necessarily imply that ice was not produced at the ice storage facility.

4 | Ice houses - typology and distribution

Initial observations

At the outset of the survey an ice house configuration like the one previously observed at Kerman, Sirjan and Abarqu was expected. At those locations the ice house components were (ref. page 4): dome, ice pit, ice ponds, shade walls, and water supply system. But already during the first day of exploration a series of variations to the expected configuration occurred, and during the following days and weeks more were to follow:

· Dome: Ice house domes turned out to have other shapes than the reverse funnel-like dome observed years ago at Abarqu (Fig. 1.2), and some domed ice house complexes had two or three domes.

· Ice House Walls: Not all ice houses had domes over the ice storage pit. Ice houses without a dome had a high, long wall on the south side of their open-air ice pits, sometimes with shorter wing walls at their eastern and western ends.

· Ice Pit: Most ice storage pits were simple excavations into the soil, with untreated wall and bottom surfaces. A few ice pits had been lined with gypsum mortar (*saruj*) for strength and sealing, and some had (dry) stone walls. In rare cases, the ice pit was built like an underground cellar, with walls and ceilings made of either mud bricks or baked bricks and with the bottom surface of stamped earth. Inspection of the ice pit floor surfaces was often not possible, either because the particular ice house was locked off (e.g. by the authorities or a farmer who used it as a common storage room), or because it was the den of wild dogs, malicious wasps, or sheep, or because the pit was full of rubbish or manure. In only two cases were the remains of a bottom drain observed in an ice pit.

- Ice Ponds: Traces of ice-making ponds were only visible at a few ice houses, in conjunction with (remains of) shade walls. Local contacts at some sites reported that ice-making had taken place in open-air, unprotected ice ponds in fields in the vicinity of ice houses.
- Shade Walls: Approximately half of the domed ice houses had associated shade walls for protection of their ice-making ponds against the sunshine and wind. The other half (about 50) had no shade walls, which meant that ice had either been produced in open unshielded ponds, or that ice had been brought in from the outside.
- Water Supply for Ice-making Ponds: Water supply systems had not been observed. During the survey it would be assessed whether water had come from natural streams (very rare) or from qanats, the underground water tunnels from the mountains, or from wells.

Another important aspect of ice houses that diverged from expectations was their location. Initially it was believed that ice houses had only served the rural communities on the fringe of the large deserts. This was, indeed, the case for the majority of them. However, special ice houses were detected that had supplied ice to towns like Tehran and Isfahan in the western part of the Project Area, and to the town of Birjand in the east. Furthermore, a limited number of ice houses belonging to caravansaries or forts, and located outside them, were found and surveyed. In other words, ice houses had served not only the populations of villages, and in some cases towns, but had also served the residents and guests of forts and caravansaries.

All ice houses dealt with here are situated in a triangle around the large central deserts, i.e. the Project Area. On the northern perimeter they are found in a narrow belt – almost like a string of pearls - from Tehran to Nishabur, at a distance of up to 20 kilometers from the Elburz mountain range. In the west, ice houses are located in a 200 kilometers wide zone between the central deserts and the Zagros Mountains. This zone contains a series of lesser deserts, still of a considerable size, separated by minor mountain ridges. In eastern Iran the ice houses are found on the eastern fringe of the Dasht-e-Kavir and its eastern extension between the 34th and 35th parallels north, and around the town of Birjand.

Some ice houses had disappeared, but I was able to confirm their former existence and possible type by one of the following means: Local contacts pinpointing the site, cultural heritage authority records, other reliable written records, as well as oral confirmation at the sites. Localization through the study of Google Earth satellite imagery confirmed several of these sites, as I have indicated in the Ice House Catalogue with all site data. The maps on pages 46 and 62 show the location of all ice houses of the survey.

Categories – Typology

Due to the significant variations in design, layout, function and client categories for the ice houses, it became necessary to devise a classification system as a basis for the development of a typology to help create order in the mass of evidence. Early in the process the survey record was expanded to include the registration of **i**) ice house superstructure/morphology, **ii**) anticipated main customer category, **iii**) availability of an ice-making plant, and **iv**) whether the ice house still existed or not. A letter symbol for each of these factors became the basis for a **four-letter classification system** and the ensuing typology.

Design/Morphology

The first letter of the classification code indicates the morphology, i.e. the design or shape of an ice house. Fig. 4.1 shows in schematic form the three different designs that were encountered during the survey:

D = Dome type ice house, with a dome over the ice storage pit, as noted at Abarqu.

W = Wall type ice house, with a tall wall(s) shielding the ice storage pit(s), as observed at Kuhpayeh and Isfahan (see later).

U = an underground ice house with a storage cellar, supplied with ice via a ramp or staircase from the ice-making pond on the north side of one or more shading walls, as reported by local contacts for Saveh and Tehran (see later).

Domed ice houses (*yakh-châl*, YC) are often confused with domed water reservoirs (*âb-anbâr*, AA). They look similar, but there are distinct differences:

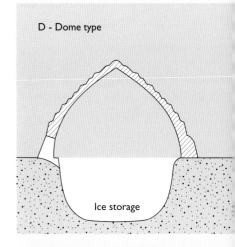

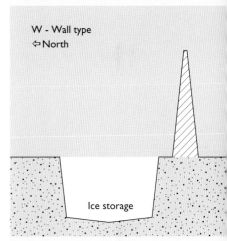

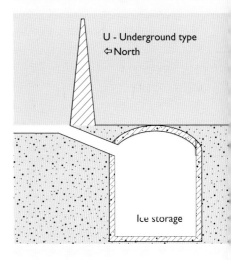

Fig. 4.1. Ice house main shapes

- AA has a staircase outside the dome, often with a porch at ground level, down to the tap at the bottom of the reservoir.
- AA often has a wind tower, *bâd-gir*, for cooling and ventilation. An ice house never has a *bâd-gir*, but most often a ventilation hole at the top of the dome.
- AA is built of baked bricks due to the humid environment, a YC (almost) never.
- YC has doors at ground level, an AA never. There is never human traffic inside an AA except during cleaning operations.
- YC usually has a ledge at ground level around the storage pit, in combination with a staircase or ladder for access to the pit. There is usually no access to an AA interior.

In many cases, abandoned water reservoirs were used for ice storage (Anaitallad et. al. 1970: 182), while the opposite could never be the case. Mud brick ice houses cannot stand humidity or water except at the bottom of the ice pit where melt water could seep away.

In *Iran - The Cradle of Civilization* (Bakhtiar and Azad 2004: 64), the authors feature photographs of two "water cisterns" near Shahrud that are in fact ice houses. They correctly label the Moayedi ice house in Kerman by its proper designation. However, this book demonstrates that there is a need to improve the general knowledge about the old traditional ice houses.

In several cases, it was difficult during the survey to decide whether an ice house had been a W-type or a U-type because the tall walls were similar, and the ice storage chamber had disappeared. In a couple of cases (Arbab Taghi/Tehran and Rahimabad/Birjand, see later), only tall walls were found and no trace of ice pits, ice cellars or ice-making ponds. However, by comparing the layout and dimensions with, for instance, the large complex at Jaffarabad, found later south of Tehran, it was concluded that the Arbab Taghi and Rahimabad ice houses most probably had had large ice cellar reservoirs, which had been demolished earlier and filled up completely without a trace. Furthermore, it was concluded that the many no longer existing town ice houses at Tehran (Khaniabad, Khalili, Ahang Street, Khorasan Square, Gholhak, and Fath Square) had been of the underground type, as indicated by Boisen (1946: 124) for the Khaniabad ice houses, which were demolished to make space for the large shunting yard of the Tehran Railway Station, built in the years 1935-1938.

When there was doubt regarding the layout or design of a particular ice house after the survey, there was (sometimes) the opportunity of checking the site layout on Google Earth. Whenever Google Earth offered a clear view of a site, a check of the layout of the site and of field measurements was undertaken.

Customers

The second code letter indicates the main user category:

V = Village ice house, having served mainly a village population, as observed in Abarqu.

C = Caravansary ice house, having served a caravansary (or a fort) and its users, as at Meybod.

T = Town ice house, having served the people of a town district, as observed in Isfahan.

Ice Manufacture

The third code letter indicates whether the ice house had an associated ice-making plant, or not:

P = an ice plant with tall pond-shading walls associated with the ice house.

O = no (visible) associated ice plant (but open-air ice-making without protecting walls still possible).

As local contacts explained, the workers at an ice house often made ice in open, unshielded shallow ponds in fields around the ice house during the frosty winter nights. This suggests that the letter O – meaning no ice-plant by definition – should really mean no shading walls on site, rather than that ice was not made. Interviews with the local guides at Kuhpayeh, between Isfahan and Nain, and at Hassan Khordu, north of Mashad (outside the Project Area), confirmed that open-field ice-making, without shading walls, was practiced there (i.e. the code letter O applied in the typology signifies absence of shading walls but not necessarily absence of ice-making!).

Fig. 4.2. Decision tree for coding of ice houses

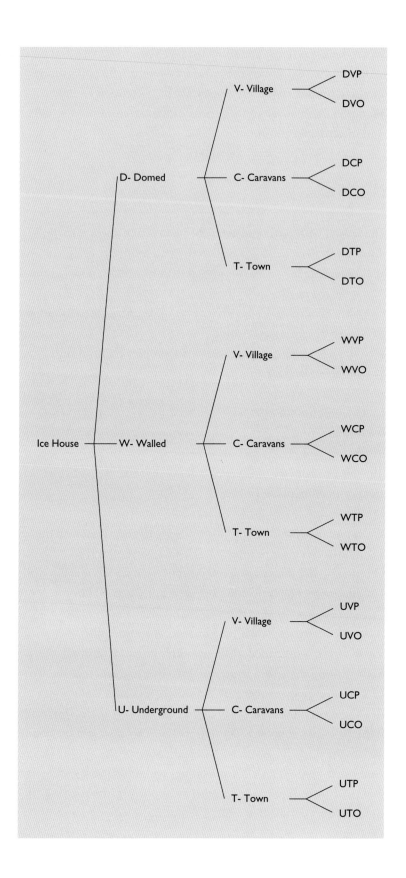

Ice House, existing (in part) or gone.

Furthermore, in order to cover the situation that an ice house site had been identified, but the ice house no longer existed, a suffix "g" (gone) was introduced.

Classification Codes.

The classification of ice houses follows the steps shown in Fig. 4.2. The coding steps upon the discovery of an ice house (YC) site were accordingly:

· Determination of type of ice house's protective structure: Dome (D), Wall (W), or Underground (U).
· Determination of type of main customer basis: Village (V), Caravansary/Fort (C), or Town (T).
· Discovery of associated ice plant (P), or not (O).
· Observation whether (remains of) ice house still existing, or gone (g).

The letter codes which came into use during the project are the following:

DVP: Domed Village ice house with an associated ice Plant.
DVPg: Domed Village ice house with ice Plant, located but no longer existing.
DVO: Domed Village ice house, nO trace of ice plant.
DVOg: Domed Village ice house, nO trace of ice plant, located/no longer exists.
DCP: Domed ice house associated with a Caravansary, with ice Plant.
DCO: Domed ice house associated with a Caravansary, nO trace of ice Plant.
UVP: Underground ice house, at a Village, with ice making Plant.
UTP: Underground ice house, at a Town, with ice-making Plant.
WVP: Walled Village ice house with ice Plant.
WVPg: Walled Village ice house with ice Plant, located/no longer exists.
WTP: Walled Town ice house with ice Plant.
WTPg: Walled Town ice house with ice Plant, located/no longer exists.

In preparation for detailed descriptions and analyses, the ice houses of the project were provided with a unique identification serial number (ID), ranging from YC·001 to YC·129, as indicated in the left column of the Ice House List in Fig. 4.3. (YC/*yakhchâl*: Ice house in Persian). As mentioned earlier, a few ice houses were identified only on the basis of literature and oral sources and could not be found or classified on the basis of knowledge obtained in the field. For such ice houses, identified but not found and/or categorized, the code XXX was applied. They were included in the Ice House List, but not provided with a serial number. These ice houses could be the subject of further search in a continuation of the present project.

List of ice houses

A total of 129 ice house sites were found, registered, codified and mapped. Only at 104 of these sites were there remains of an ice house to be found, i.e. on 25 sites no trace of the ice house was anymore to be found. None of the ice house installations located in the survey was 100% complete. The ice houses had often suffered heavy damage, ice-making ponds had disappeared with only a few traces left, and water supply systems had disappeared completely.

The existence of a further 10 ice houses was indicated by reliable sources (e.g. the National Registry, appraisal reports of the Cultural Heritage Organization, references in the literature, or local contacts) but they could not be found and classified. Several of these are believed to have disappeared, but they are included in the Ice House List with the code XXX due to the uncertainty concerning their shape, users, layout and existence.

The main results of the field work, complemented by data such as registration number and proposed age from the National Registry, are presented in the table in Fig. 4.3 (i.e. 4.3A, 4.3B, and 4.3C), List of Ice Houses Located in the Project Area. The Ice House List constitutes the most important document of the ice house project as it contains all main survey data and the first derivatives. The Ice House List is supported and complemented by the Ice House Catalogue of the original dissertation.

For each ice house visited or identified with certainty, the following main data – to the extent they were available - are listed in Fig. 4.3:

ID No.   Project identification serial number, i.e. YC·No.

N.R.   National Registry serial number for the province con-
              cerned. For example, T564 means No. 564 in Tehran
              Province, and so forth.

WP No.   Way Point number used during field work.

Prov.name   Name of province at the top of the names of the sites in
              that province.

Shahrestan   Name of county within the province.

Location   Name of location.

North   Northern latitude in degrees, in WSP 1984 Global Sys-
              tem.

East   Eastern longitude in degrees, in WSP 1984 Global Sys-
              tem.

Elev.   Site elevation above sea level (ASL), in meters.

Cat.   Category of ice house expressed in Project Code Sys-
              tem.

Age   Historic era of building (Safavid Dynasty 1491-1722,
              Qadjar Dynasty 1796-1925, Recent means post-1925),
              usually taken from the National Registry (Pazooki, N.,
              and A. Shadmehr 2005).

Photos Nos.   Numbers of the photographs taken by the author. A
              few references to other sources, e.g. Google Earth im-
              agery.

A full account of the survey findings – including all relevant photographs taken during the field work - is contained in "Catalogue of
Ice Houses in the Project Area" of the original dissertation.

Fig. 4.4 shows the locations of all ice houses surveyed – regardless of type or code – plotted onto a map of Iran. From a group of
several ice houses in the Tehran area at the northwest corner of the
project area triangle a line of ice houses sites stretches eastwards towards Mashad and then southwards to a concentration around the
town of Birjand in East Iran. In the western part of the project area
the ice houses are located in a wide band in a southeastern direction,
ending at the town of Bam with its famous citadel (Arg-e-Bam),
both severely damaged in a severe earthquake on 26th December
2003. On that occasion the restored ice house of the Arg also partly
collapsed, more to follow later.

ID No.	N.R.	WP No.	Province name	Shahrestan	Location	North
	THR	**I**	**Tehran Prov.**		**Tehran**	
1		87	Arbab Taghi	Tehran	Kh. Takhti	35 39,644
2			Khaniabad	Tehran	Railway St. Area	35 39,350
3	T059		Khalili	Tehran	Kh. 17. Shahrivar	35 41,000
			Imamz. Davoud	Tehran		
4		31	Kh. Ahang	Tehran	Shahidayiat A.M.	35 40,544
5		29	M.Khorasan	Tehran	M.Korasan	35 39,955
6			Gholhak	Tehran	Kh. Yakhchal	35 46,440
7		32	Kan	Tehran	Kan Suburb	35 45,578
8			M.Fat'h	Tehran	Old Karaj Road	35 40,700
		103	Shah Abdol Azim	Shahr Rey	Shahr Rey	35 35,200
9		105	Hezar Zurgh	Varamin	Varamin	35 13,700
10	T564	139	Tarshanbeh	Islamshahr	BakhshChaDang	35 35,792
11	T565	44	Aliaabad	Islamshahr	Aliabad Village	35 36,768
12		138	Hakimabad	Islamshahr	Hakimabad V.	35 28,487
13		140	Robat Karim	Robat Karim	Robat Karim	35 28,497
14		141	Vahnabad	Robat Karim	Vahnabad V.	35 26,791
15		142	Jaffarabad Jangal	Shahr Rey	Jaffarabad V.	35 33,656
16			Arad	Hassanabad	Arad V.	35 20,000
17		104	Koleyn	Hassanabad	Koleyn V.	35 20,356
	QOM	**2**	**Qom Prov.**		**Tehran**	
18		49	Taghrud	Qom	Taghrud East	34 44,394
	MAR	**3**	**Markazi Prov.**		**Arak**	
19		99	Saveh	Saveh	Karkhaneh Ghand	35 00.950
20	C158	100	Mehdiabad	Zarandieh	Khorshidabad V.	35 16,351
	KER	**22**	**Kerman Prov.**		**Kerman**	
21	K092	82	Ravar	Ravar	Ravar Center	31 16,401
22			Zarand	Zarand		30 49,200
23	Kxxx		Anar	Anar	Anar	30 52,820
24	K064		Hadj Ali Agha	Rafsanjan	Abassabad V.	30 30,000
25			Kabutar Khan	Rafsanjan	Kabutar Khan V.	30 16,620
26	K087		Moayeri	Kerman	Kh. Abu Hamed	30 17,715
27			Rigabad	Kerman	Rigabad V.	30 16,880
28	K102		Zarisf/Asa'i Sefid	Kerman	Kh. Zarisf	30 17,670
29	K190		Djo Moyedi	Kerman	Kh. Sam	30 17,000
30	K341		Langar	Kerman	Langar/Mahan V.	30 4,550
31	K194	78	Bam Castle	Bam	Arg-e-Bam	29 7,007
32	K294	83	Sirjan	Sirjan		29 27,204
33		85	Mahmoudabad	Sirjan	Mahmoudabad V.	29 31,558
	YAZ	**23**	**Yazd Prov.**		**Yazd**	
34	Y054	5	Meybod	Ardekan	Meybod	32 13,630
35			Yazd	Yazd	Yazd	31 54,000
	Y227		Fathabad	Fathabad	Fathabad V.	
36			Taft	Taft	Taft	31 44,500
	Y367		Benderabad	Sadough	Benderabad V.	
37	Y288	7	Abarqu I/Agha	Abarqu	Main Road	31 7,465
38		11	Abarqu II	Abarqu	NW of town	31 7,759
39	Y253	9	Hek/Abarqu III	Abarqu	Near Hek V.	31 6,608

Fig. 4.3A. List of ice houses in Project Area - Part 1

East	Elevation m.	Category	Age	Photos No.	Remarks
51 24,665	1130	UTP		1118-27	Restored/Modified
51 24,050	1100	UTPg			Boisen (1946:124) - Gone 1936
51 27,000	1180	UTPg	Recent		Presumed Gone
		XXX			No Data. Gone
51 25,831	1154	UTPg			Gone
51 26,716	1166	UTPg			Gone
51 26,340	1440	UTPg			Gone
51 16,859	1419	WTP		484-493	
51 20,400	1160	UTPg			Gone
51 26,100	1051	XXX		1286-88	Gone. No Data
51 44,562	861	DVPg			Gone 30-40 years ago
51 15,490	1100	DVO	Safavid	1622-25	1630-31 from Museum, Qadjar
51 14,413	1117	DVP	Qadjar	525-534	1632-34 from Museum
51 12,655	1029	DVP		1616-21	
51 4,667	1049	DVP		1636-40	Long Walls
51 10,509	1016	UVP		1641-43	Hossein Village
51 18,900	1061	UTP		1644-58	The "Cathedral"
51 16,000	950	DVPg		1289-90	Gone
51 18,201	951	DVP		1291-1297	Shelter+Hamam nearby
50 31,409	1033	UVP		546-563	Maybe C-Use
50 21,707	1019	UTPg			Gone
50 32,258	1284	DVO	Qadjar	1267-73	
56 48,094	1189	DVP	Qadjar	961-981	
56 33,000	1650	DVPg			Gone. Site not Found.
55 15,820	1406	DVP		472-480	NR No. on Missing Page
56 00.000	1490	DVP	Qadjar	465-471	
56 20,714	1685	DVP		457-464	
57 4,003	1758	DVP	Safavid	423-430	
57 4,860	1762	DVP	Safavid	440-442	
57 5,965	1761	DVP	Qadjar	431-438	946-951, One Year Later
57 5,000	1760	DVPg	Qadjar		Not Found. Gone?
57 16,030	1860	DVP	Qadjar	443-453	
58 22,338	1053	DCP	Safavid/Qadjar	939-945	Add. Photos 683-686
55 39,711	1731	DVP	Qadjar	983-993	2 Domes
55 36,214	1706	DVP		994-1017	
54 00.515	1120	DCP	Safavid	138-148	401-407
54 35,000	1480	DVPg			Gone
		XXX	Qadjar		Site not Found.
54 11,000	1555	DVPg			Gone
		XXX	Qadjar		No Visit - Type DVP Presumed
53 16,589	1517	DVP	Qadjar	155-166	
53 14,900	1524	DVP	Qadjar	167-192	Maleknia Family
53 15,754	1523	DVP	Qadjar	204-217	

ID No.	N.R.	WP No.	Province name	Shahrestan	Location	North
	ISF	24	Isfahan Prov.		Isfahan	
40	1697	47	Mazreh Drum	Kashan	S of Meshkan	34 6,413
41		48	Nazrabad	Kashan	New Mosque	34 5,595
42		16	Moayedi I	Kashan	Kashan	33 58,363
43		17	Moayedi II	Kashan	Kashan	33 58,368
44		19	Kashan Town	Kashan	Kashan	33 59,000
45		24	Mahabad	Ardestan	Mahabad V.	33 31,474
46		23	Zavareh	Ardestan	Zavareh V.	33 27,038
47		22	Ardestan	Ardestan		33 22,400
48		13	Kh.Ateshgah I	Isfahan	Isfahan	32 39,569
49		14	Kh.Ateshgah II	Isfahan	Isfahan	32 39,204
50			Gorat	Isfahan	Gorat V.	32 40,000
51		1	Kuhpayeh I	Isfahan	Kuhpayeh	32 42,581
52		2	Kuhpayeh II	Isfahan	Kuhpayeh	32 42,335
53	1652	x03	Tariqi Nain	Nain	Mahaleh Kalavan	32 51,876
			Shahreza I	Shareza	Shahreza	32 00.000
			Abadeh	Abadeh	Abadeh	31 9,270
	SEM	25	Semnan Prov.		Semnan	
54		75	Hos.abad Kheleh	Garmsar	Hoseinabad V.	35 13,537
55		110	Ghahtul Bozorg	Garmsar	Ghahtul V.	35 11,986
56		110	Ghahtul Kuchek	Garmsar	Ghahtul V.	35 11,986
57		108	Rikan	Garmsar	Rikan V.	35 11,377
58		111	Kardovan	Garmsar	Kardovan V.	35 11,012
59		114	Shah Sefid	Garmsar	Shahsefid V.	35 11,001
60		113	Sudaghlan	Garmsar	Sudaghlan V.	35 10,864
61		98	Yahteri	Aradan	Yahteri Sefli V.	35 11,784
62		97	Padeh	Aradan	Padeh V.	35 15,091
63		112	Imamz.Zoalefqar	Garmsar	Imamzadeh Zoal.	35 11,857
64	S272	73	Dah Namak	Garmsar	Dah Namak V.	35 15,342
65		74	Dah Namak Old	Garmsar	Dah Namak V.	35 15,204
66			Lasjerd	Semnan	Sidabad V.	35 25,300
67		71	Sarkheh	Semnan	Sarkheh	35 28,181
68	S273		Sarkheh I	Semnan	Sarkheh	35 27,700
69			Biabanak	Semnan	Sarkheh	35 24,840
70	S276	66	Zaveghan	Semnan	Zavegan	35 33,757
71	S279		Shah Djugh Kuch	Semnan	E of Railway	35 34,250
72	S289		Shah Djugh Boz.	Semnan	W of Railway	35 33,878
73	S282	68	Ateshgah	Semnan	Abu Zar	35 33,516
74	S288	69	Maheleh Chup	Semnan		35 33,770
75		94	Firouzabad	Damghan	Firouzabad V.	35 58,086
76			Abdolabad	Damghan	Abdolabad V.	35 56,725
77		136	Alyan	Damghan	Alyan V.	35 54,824
78			Mohamad-Abadu	Damghan	Moh.-Abadu V.	36 00.192
79		134	Forat	Damghan	Forat V.	35 55,593
80		135	Hassanabad	Damghan	Hassanabad V.	35 54,941
81		133	Jaffarabad	Damghan	Jaffarabad V.	36 6,859
82		130	Shamsabad	Damghan	Shamsabad V.	36 7,847
83		131	Berum	Damghan	Berum V.	36 8,589
84		132	Vamerzan	Damghan	Vamerzan V.	36 10,650
85		137	Qaleh Agha Baba	Damghan	Damghan	36 9,165

Fig. 4.3B. List of ice houses in Project
Area - Part II

East	Elevation m.	Category	Age	Photos No.	Remarks
51 18,961	897	DVP	Safavid	537-544	
51 21,071	891	DVPg			Gone. Was Bibizeynab?
51 26,490	970	DCP		240-245	
51 26,529	969	DCP		246-254	
51 23,200	1003	DVPg			Min. 5 Nos. All Gone
52 12,977	1014	DVO		267-268	
52 29,822	990	DVP		262-266	
52 22,100	1207	DVPg		258-261	Gone
51 38,105	1600	WTP		220-230	
51 31,561	1608	WTPg		232	Gone
51 50,000	1550	WVP			No Visit - Type WVP Presumed
52 25,856	1785	WVP		118-120	
52 26,657	1788	WVP		124-129	
53 5,617	1573	DVP	Qadjar	133-134	
51 50,000		XXX			2 Nos. - Gone
52 39,556	2017	XXX			1 No. - Gone
52 19,115	863	DVOg			Gone
52 23,369	881	DVO		1397-1404	
52 23,369	881	DVO		1397-1404	
52 23,467	871	DVO		1387-1394	Half - Burned
52 24,187	865	DVOg		1405	Gone. Photo in MF Book
52 26,307	862	DVO		1417-19	Photo in MF Book
52 28,746	847	DVO		1411-16	
52 29,170	861	DVO		1264-66	
52 32,222	856	DVO		1260-63	
52 32,884	827	DVO		1406-10	Photo in MF Book
52 43,868	840	DCO	Qadjar	713-717	
52 43,953	833	DCO		723-730	
53 5,800	1223	DCO			Seen from Bus. Uncertain
53 13,305	1159	DVP		709-710	Dome Gone?
53 12,805	1137	DVO	Qadjar		Possible main YC of Sark
53 16,135	1037	DVO			9 km S of Sarkheh
53 21,884	1152	DVO	Qadjar	687-692	
53 24,911	1124	DVOg	Qadjar	Google Earth	Presumed Gone
53 24,585	1111	DVO	Qadjar	Google Earth	
53 24,092	1121	DVO	Qadjar	697-700	
53 24,570	1128	DVO	Qadjar	701-708	
54 10,350	1181	DVP		1245-54	
54 11,480	1167	DVP			
54 17,702	1114	DVO		1577-83	S of Town, near Arg
54 17,824	1092	DVO		1588-91	E of Arg with Square Tower
54 18,723	1121	DVO		1557-61	In Garden, via House
54 19,400	1106	DVO		1562-71	In Cemetery
54 21,926	1114	DVO		1541-56	Near large Arg
54 23,732	1105	DVO		1520-25	
54 25,299	1103	DVO		1526-35	
54 26,034	1110	DVO		1537-40	
54 22,020	1146	DVO		1591-93	Converted into Garage

ID No.	N.R.	WP No.	Province name	Shahrestan	Location	North
	SEM	**25**	**Semnan Prov.**	**Semnan**		
86			Djizan South	Damghan	S of Djizan	36 12,043
87			Imamabad	Damghan	S of Mehmandsh	36 12,230
88	S295	42	Bedasht	Shahrud	Behdasht Village	36 25,349
89		43	Bedasht II	Shahrud	Behdasht V.	36 25,373
90	S306	129	Sa'adabad	Shahrud	Sa'adabad V.	36 24,132
91	S380	40	Agha Mhm Lotfi	Shahrud	Dizedj V.	36 21,769
92		41	Dizedj Central	Shahrud	Dizedj V.	36 21,650
93			Garman	Shahrud	Garman V.	36 37,610
94			Mianabad	Shahrud	Mianabad V.	36 30,000
95			Zargar	Shahrud	Zargar V.	36 35,500
96			Chahar Taq	Shahrud	Chahar Taq V.	36 36,000
97	S404	124	Biar Djamand	Shahrud	Biar Djamand V.	36 4,417
98	S395		Jilan	Shahrud	Jilan V.	36 35,500
99	S396	38	Mazdj	Shahrud	Mazdj V.	36 37,332
100		36	Azamabad	Shahrud	Azamabad V.	36 35,305
101	S305		Dowlatabad Mo'j	Shahrud	Dowlatabad V.	36 31,000
102		127	Hawa'i	Shahrud	Bostam North	36 29,765
103		126	Bostam	Shahrud	At Telecom Cplx	36 29,046
104	S307	39	Ghasemabad	Shahrud	N of Bostam	36 30,205
	S313		H Mahmoud T S	Shahrud	W of Bostam	
			Karbala'i	Shahrud	Bostam Town	
			Yusef Karbala'i	Shahrud	Bostam Town	
105		125	Miami	Shahrud	Miami	36 24,695
106		89	Abbasabad	Shahrud	Abassabad V.	36 21,398
107		90	Sadrabad	Shahrud	Sadrabad V.	36 21,770
	RKH	**29**	**R. Khorasan Prov.**	**Mashad**		
108	R238	92	Sabzevar I	Sabzevar	Sabzevar	36 11,760
109	R310	91	Sabzevar II	Sabzevar	Sabzevar	36 12,010
110			Maidan Gusfand	Sabzevar	Sabzevar	36 11,500
111		93	Zafaranieh	Sabzevar	Zafaranieh	36 9,977
112		120	Ardoghesh	Nishabur	Ardoghesh V.	36 8,473
113		121	Behrud	Nishabur	Behrud V.	36 14,223
			Dowlatabad	Nishabur		
114	R548	122	Soltanabad	Sabzevar	Soltanabad	36 24,332
115	R299	x58	Kashmar	Kashmar	Ferotegheh V.	35 13,210
116	R719	57	Khaf	Khaf	Khaf	34 34,322
117	R885		Sangan	Khaf	Sangan/Khaf	34 23,970
118		59	Amrani	Gonabad	Amrani Caravans	34 33,447
119		60	Amrani Fortress	Gonabad	Amrani Fortress	34 33,478
120		64	Najmabad	Gonabad	Najmabad V.	34 13,010
121	R749	62	Rahen	Gonabad	Rahen V.	34 20,314
122	R221	63	Kowsar	Gonabad	Bidokht V.	34 21,612
	SKH	**30**	**S. Khorasan Prov.**		**Birjand**	
123	J004	54	Shokatabad	Birjand	3 km SE of Birj.	32 51,404
124	J044	56	Behlgerd	Birjand	Behlgerd V.	32 47,026
125	J244	x50	Rahimabad	Birjand	Rahimabad St.	32 50,769
126		51	Amirabad-Sheiv.	Birjand	Amirab.-Sheivani	32 50,211
127		52	Birjand SE Twin	Birjand		32 50,657
128		55	Bojd	Birjand	Bojd V.	32 50,419
129		65	Moalem/Khayam	Birjand	Kh.Khayam	32 51,267

Fig. 4.3C. List of ice houses in Project
Area - Part III

East	Elevation m.	Category	Age	Photos No.	Remarks
54 23,483	1134	DVO		Google Earth	Seen from Bus
54 33,340	1089	DVO		Google Earth	Driver Info
55 3,215	1304	DVO	Qadjar	514-517	
55 3,161	1304	DVO		518-525	
55 2,866	1293	DVP	Qadjar	1518-1519	
55 1,092	1272	DVO	Qadjar	512-513	
55 1,046	1272	DVOg		No Photo	Gone. Piece of Wall only
55 3,462	1444	DVO		Google Earth	Photo in MF Book
55 2,000	1410	DVOg			MF Book. No Data.
55 6,000	1400	DVOg			MF Book. No Data.
55 6,000	1440	DVOg			MF Book. No Data.
55 48,385	1106	DVO	Qadjar	1489-1495	
55 33,200	1100	DVP	Qadjar		Road Closed, No Visit
55 22,828	1308	DVP	Qadjar	498-503	
55 4,750	1410	DVO		495-497	
55 00.650	1400	DVO	Qadjar	1513-17	
55 00.270	1419	DVP			Dome Gone, Trace on GE
54 59,474	1453	DVP		1505-11	
55 00.784	1409	DVO		504-511	
		XXX	Qadjar		No Visit - Dome Presumed
		XXX			Karbala'i Niza Halva'i
		XXX			Yusef Karbala'i Reza Qoli
55 38,975	1098	DVO		1496-1502	2 Domes. In Martyr Cemetry
56 23,360	956	DCO		1204-08	
56 33,961	827	DCO		1209	
57 39,732	954	DVP	Qadjar	1222-32	3 Domes (895+899)
57 39,291	960	DVP	Qadjarj	1210-21	2 of 3 Domes Gone
57 39,820	938	DVP		1240-44	Now Teahouse
58 5,238	1045	DCP		1233-39	Beazley Photo
58 57,944	1258	DVO		1459-1465	
58 33,181	1136	DVO		1466-1477	P, but No Wall
		XXX			No Visit
58 2,069	1214	DVO	Pahlavi	1478-1487	At Arg - One More IceH Gone
58 29,266	1061	DVP	Qadjar	625-634	
60 8,923	978	DVP	Qadjar	616-623	
60 15,060	863	DVP	Safavid-Qadjar		No Visit
58 42,179	919	DCO		635-636	
58 42,667	919	DCO		637-641	
58 48,034	1239	DVO		652-654	
58 39,022	1136	DVO	Qadjar	645-649	Later Converted into AA
58 45,558	1062	DVOg	Qadjar	650-651	
59 17,335	1510	DVP	Qadjar	587-596	
59 23,054	1815	DVP	Qadjar	602 611	
59 13,258	1522	UTP	Qadjar	679-682	Presumed U-Type, +566 & 572
59 11,459	1595	DVP		567-571	
59 15,160	1514	DVP		573-586	2 Domes
59 19,041	1562	DVP		597-601	
59 13,686	1489	DVO		612-615	

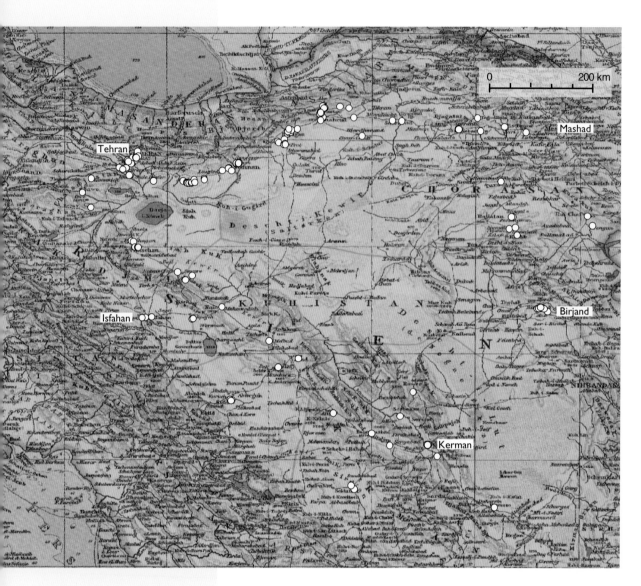

Fig. 4.4. Map with all surveyed ice house sites. (map from Koppels Forlag, c. 1925)

Distribution by altitude

Concentrations of ice houses were found in the countryside in the vicinity of the towns of Tehran (Altitude 950-1420 meters above sea level; 9 examples), Kerman (1760 m; 3), Abarqu (1520 m; 3), Isfahan (1600 m; 5), Garmsar (100 km east of Tehran - 850 m; 10), Semnan (1120 m; 4), Shahrud (1300 m; 5), Sabzevar (950 m; 3), and Birjand (1520 m; 6). A graphic illustration of the ice house elevations in the involved provinces is shown in Fig. 4.5. The concentrations are reflected in the columns for the provinces of Tehran, Kerman, Yazd, Isfahan, Semnan (which includes the Garmsar area), and the two Khorasan provinces.

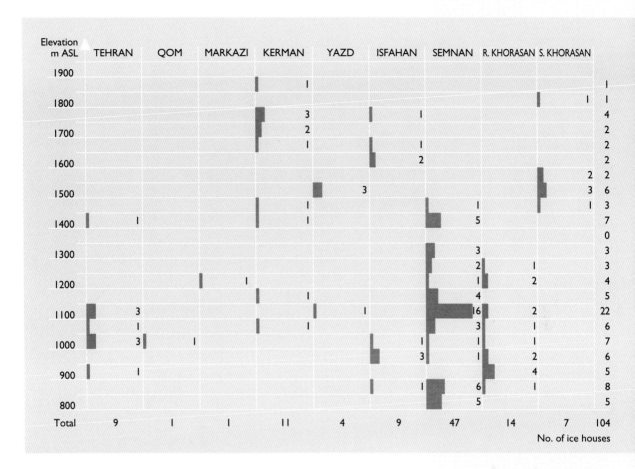

Fig. 4.5. Ice house elevations in provinces

Fig. 4.5 shows that there is considerable variation in the altitude of the Iranian ice houses, as such. The diagram further indicates that a correlation between concentrations of ice houses and particular elevations is probably irrelevant. The local climate, the soil conditions, and the availability of water – or of natural ice in the nearby mountains – appear to be the deciding factors for the location of both villages and ice houses, in general, and also for particular types of ice houses. To these factors can be added social ones in the form of demand and relative wealth of the community served by the ice houses.

Distribution by province

The distribution of ice houses by province is shown in the table in Fig. 4.6. As has been noted, the total number of ice house sites identified is 129, of which no trace of the installation remained at 25 of them.

TYPE/PROV	TEHRAN	QOM	MARKAZI	KERMAN	YAZD	ISFAHAN	SEMNAN	R. KHORASAN	S. KHORASAN	TOTAL
DVP	4 + 2			10 + 2	3 + 2	3 + 3	8 + 0	6 + 0	5 + 0	39 + 9
DVO	1 + 0		1+0			1 + 0	34 + 7	5 + 1	1 + 0	43 + 8
DCP				1 + 0	1 + 0	2 + 0		1 + 0		5 + 0
DCO							5 + 0	2 + 0		7 + 0
DTP										
DTO										
WVP						3 + 0				3 + 0
WVO										
WCP										
WCO										
WTP	1 + 0					1 + 1				2 + 1
WTO										
UVP	1 + 0	1 + 0								2 + 0
UVO										
UCP										
UCO										
UTP	2 + 6		0 + 1						1 + 0	3 + 7
UTO										
Total 1	9 + 8	1 + 0	1 + 1	11 + 2	4 + 2	10 + 4	47 + 7	14 + 1	7 + 0	104 + 25
Total 2	17	1	2	13	6	14	54	15	7	129
xxx-Unknown	2			2		2	3	1		10

Fig. 4.6. Distribution of ice houses by province

The table shows the number of ice houses, existing or disappeared (shown as, for example, 2+1), which have been visited during the survey. It further shows the number of ice houses, in total 10, which on the basis of existing sources are assumed to exist, but have not yet been located or visited (with the designation XXX). The occurrence of desert rim village ice houses has been reasonably well mapped during the survey, and enables a degree of qualitative frequency calculations and frequency analyses. This is not the case for the town ice houses and the caravansary/fort ice houses; however, despite the few examples, a lot has been learned about the latter two categories. So, while these numbers, and the data in the original ice house catalogue, may not be sufficient to allow a statistical analysis, comparisons will be made anyway to obtain partial conclusions.

The total number of ice houses identified in each province is shown on the map in Fig. 4.7 (Qom Province is not marked separately; on the map it is included in Markazi Province). Semnan Province has the largest number of ice houses, 54 in total, of which 46 are domed ice houses without a (visible) ice-making plant. 41

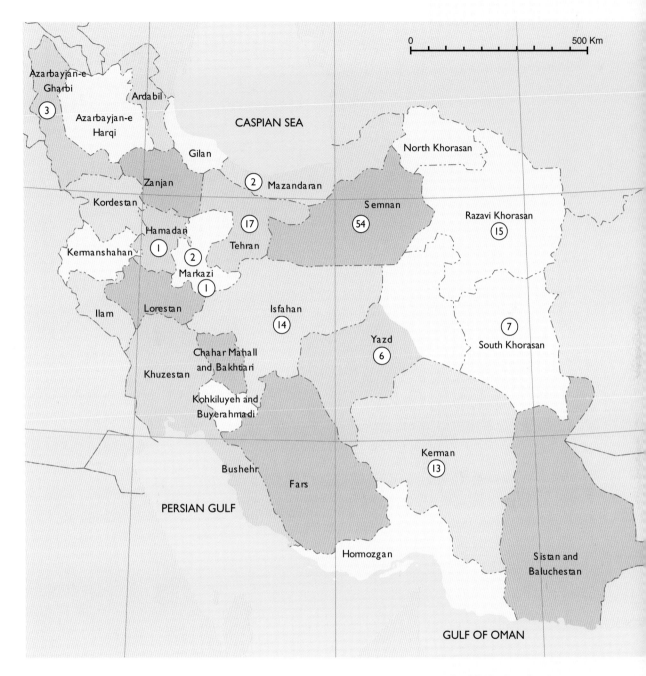

Fig. 4.7. Number of ice house sites identified during the project in each province

domed ice houses are located at villages and 5 at caravansaries. The simple reason for this high number is that Semnan Province has the longest (500 kilometers) ice house-suited zone of all provinces, i.e. with alluvial slopes and plains, and potential ice quarries nearby in the Elburz Mountains.

As already noted, the small numbers in the Tehran and Isfahan town areas, where local sources indicate that the number once was

Fig. 4.8. Decision tree for coding of ice houses

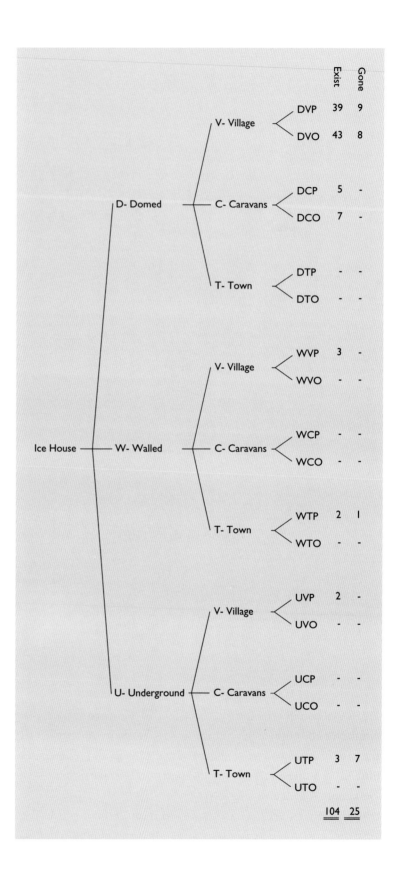

more than eighty and forty, respectively, is due to the expanding need for land for the growing population, the "urban crawl" as Dabaieh puts it (2009: 29), and at the same time the complete absence of interest for preservation of the industrial cultural heritage. Of the 20 ice house sites that existed some 80 years ago in central Tehran, described by Motamedi (2002: 715), not one appears to have survived.

The absence of ice houses with particular code letter combinations (DTP, DTO, WVO, WCP, WCO, WTO, UVO, UCP, UCO and UTO) in the decision tree model in Fig. 4.8 allows, with some certainty, the following interpretations:

- No DTPs and DTOs: Domed ice houses probably were not used in towns; they served either villages or caravansaries/forts. Town ice houses were of the wall or underground type. It may be concluded that all large commercial or industrial ice plants were of the latter types.
- No WVOs: No walled ice houses served villages, and walled ice houses usually had an associated ice-making plant.
- No WCPs and WCOs: Caravansaries and forts had only domed ice houses, probably because this type was compact and easier to operate and defend than the other more open types.
- Two UVPs and no UVO: Underground ice houses at villages were rare. Only underground ice houses with ice-making plants served villages and they were few in number.
- No UCPs and UCOs: There were no underground ice houses at caravansaries and forts, but there may well have been underground ice houses (cellars) inside the outer walls, in a manner similar to their water reservoirs. No search was carried out inside the caravansaries in order to confirm this.
- No UTOs: No underground town ice houses without ice plant were found, i.e. the large underground ice houses in and near towns (i.e. Tehran) probably all had associated ice plants.

Fig. 4.9. illustrates the distribution of ice house types in the Survey Area. Not all individual plots are visible due to several overlaps in the case of closely situated ice houses. The outline of a pattern for domed ice houses – DVO and DCO types mainly in the north and DVP and DCP mainly in the southwest – is clearly visible. This notable discovery will be analyzed and discussed in some detail later.

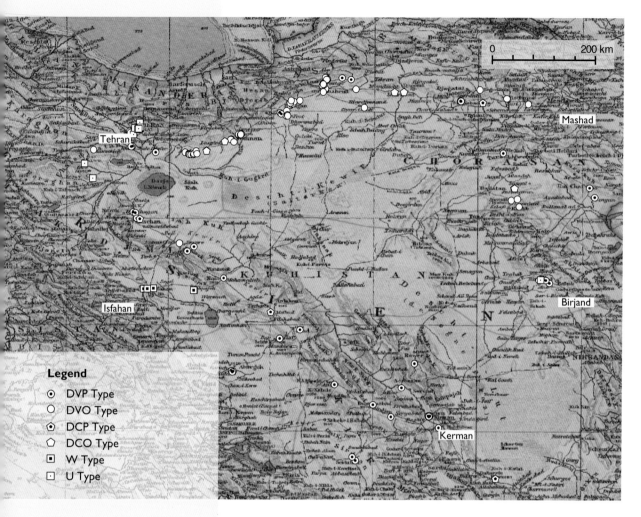

Fig. 4.9. Ice house map.

Legend
- ⊙ DVP Type
- ○ DVO Type
- ⊘ DCP Type
- ⬠ DCO Type
- ▣ W Type
- ▢ U Type

Ice Houses outside the Project Area

A number of ice houses situated outside the Project Area were also located. They are mentioned here for the interest they may have for further research:

- Radkan ice house (36 48N, 59 00E, elevation 1204 m, type DVO), 75 km northwest of Mashad, located on Google Earth.
- Chahar Borj ice house (36 27.7N 59 28.5E, elevation 1046 m, type DVO), 15 km northwest of Mashad, visited. This ice house is in the National Register.
- Hassan Khordu ice house (36 26.6N 59 30.2E, elevation 1020 m, type DVO), 10 km northeast of Mashad, visited. At this ice house a local guide (age around 60) explained how ice was made in ponds in the adjoining field, without shading walls.

- There were reports of a nearby ice house, now demolished, at Esmailabad (36 25.5N 59.30.7, elevation 1020 m, type DVO).
- Nimvar ice house (33 45N 50 35E, elevation 21025 m, type DVP), 85 km west of Kashan, visited.
- Malayer ice house (Burke 2009:206), not visited.
- In Shahmirzad (35 46N, 53 21E), in the mountains 40 kilometers to the north of Semnan, a small ice house with an external layer of rocks in cement mortar over the mud brick superstructure was found on a steep north slope. It was privately owned and nowadays used as a granary.

Additionally, during a visit to Qazvin, which is situated outside the Project Area, the cultural heritage authorities informed me that there had once been at least five ice houses in the town vicinity. Local people I met in Abadeh and Shahreza informed me that the local ice houses (one and two, respectively) had earlier been demolished and the sites built over. Hourcade (1994: 95) reported on a huge commercial ice house facility at Jaban (35 39N, 52 15E), some 80 km east of Tehran, in the Elburz Mountains. It supplied large quantities of ice to the metropolis and other towns in the area. Beazley described a particular ice house she saw at Kelisan, near Isfahan (Beazley, E., and M. Harverson 1982: 110). It was an ice house pit located in the shade of a battery of sixteen linked pigeon towers, i.e. a WVP type. A fruitless search and enquiries in the area in May 2009 indicated that this installation had been demolished about two years earlier. Finally, a tourist guide book about the area of Jolfa, in northwest Iran on the border to Armenia, confirmed the existence of an ice house at a convent complex by the name of Kordasht.

The National Register indicates ice houses at the following locations outside the Project Area, with their NR province registration number in brackets:

- Aleq Beik Ghadjur Aleq Beik (W198) – Urumieh Noh Peleh (W242) – Chores (W843), in West Azerbaijan Province.
- Chahar Borj (R584, visited during the survey) - Karimabad (R585) - Nomad Maleha (R653), in the northern part of Razavi Khorasan Province.
- Tapeh Shomali (M213) – Tapeh Djonobi (M218), at Hoseinabad, in Mazandaran Province.
- Mir Fatah (H082), Hamadan, in Hamadan Province.

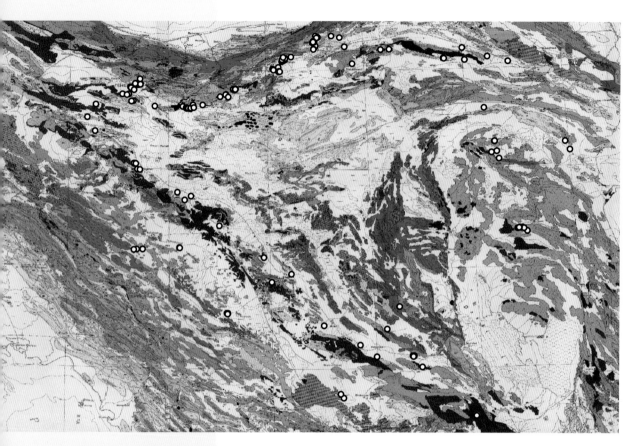

Fig. 4.10. Geological map of Iran with ice house sites. (National Iranian Oil Company, 1957)

Environmental interfaces

Topography – Geology – Soils

The analyses below are all based on plots of exact ice house locations on maps of small scale, 1:2.5 million or smaller. The observations and interpretations are therefore to be considered indicative only. In a future phase it is envisaged to refine and improve the analyses on the basis of the more exact topographical maps, which were obtained from the National Iranian Geographical Organization during the survey.

All ice houses in the Project Area were found to be situated on alluvial deposits, at altitudes varying between 830 meters above sea level in the western desert fringe and over 1800 meters in the Kerman area in the southern zone. They were all located in or adjacent to areas which were or had been under irrigation. In geological terms the ice houses were situated on quaternary formations, i.e. layers of young geological origin, which are the light-colored areas on Fig. 4.10.

Quaternary formations were deposited after the latest glacial period, which in Iran took place some 20,000 years ago. But in reality the deposits of the Project Area are much later due to the constant fluvial action originating in the surrounding mountains, and aeolian action on the Iranian Plateau.

The ice houses plotted on the morphological map in Fig. 4.11 confirm the pattern that all sites are located in "areas of frequent alluvial fan activity"[23] within the general area of "piedmonts and alluvial fan aprons, intra-montane basins and broad valley floors".[24]

The UN Food and Agriculture Organization carried out a series of soil studies in Iran in the years between 1955 and 1961 in support of modern development plans for the agricultural sector. The result, *The Soils of Iran* (Dewan and Famouri 1964), included the assessment of land use expressed in terms of soil potentiality as a basis for agricultural development. Five broad groupings were set up in order to indicate the limitations of soils for agricultural activity (1964: 17):

Group 1: Soils with no limitations or slight limitations, except possible local problems.

Group 2: Soils with slight to moderate limitations, due to either (a) moderate deficit of water or (b) due to slope, depth, water or drainage limitations.

Group 3: Soils with moderate to severe limitations, due to either (a) moderate to strong deficit of water or (b) due to slope, depth or water limitations.

Group 4: Soils with severe to very severe limitations, due to either (a) slope, depth or water limitations or (b) salinity, gravel, depth, and strong deficit of water.

Group 5: Soils with almost no potentiality, due to either (a) sand dunes or (b) salt marsh, sulfurous and gypsiferous soils (i.e., poor in nitrogen and phosphorus).

The five soil groups are shown in very general terms in Fig. 4.12.[25] Within the Project Area, and on a general scale, the best soils (Group 1) are found around Isfahan and Kerman. Group 2 soils prevail in the areas of Islamshahr, Anar, Rafsanjan, Meybod and Garmsar. Group 3 soils are found around South Tehran, Abarqu, Kashan, East Semnan, Damghan, Shahrud, Khaf and Gonabad. Soils around Sarkheh and West Semnan, Sabzevar and Birjand all belong to Group 4. In-

Fig. 4.11. Soil morphology map of Iran with ice house sites. (Iran National Geographical Organization, 1995)

ferior Group 5 soils are found locally in Kashan and around Birjand.

This picture of soil potentiality is largely confirmed by the "Soil Map of Iran" (appended to Dewan and Famouri 1964), Fig. 4.13, which provides an overview of the main soil types in the Project Area:

- Fine-textured alluvial soils: South and Southeast Tehran, Isfahan, Kerman.
- Slightly saline alluvial soils: Anar, Rafsanjan, East Garmsar.
- Plateau soils, Sierozem type: Sirjan, Abarqu, Kashan, Nain, Semnan, Damghan, Shahrud, Sabzevar, Khaf, Birjand. Sierozem soils are often slightly saline, calcareous and very humus-deficient. The agricultural value of such soil depends on suitable irrigation.
- Desert soils, occasional sand dunes: Ravar, Meybod, Gonabad.

There is no obvious pattern in the distribution of ice house sites in relation to the potentiality of the soils. The soil maps are all in small scale and the plotted positions of the ice houses must

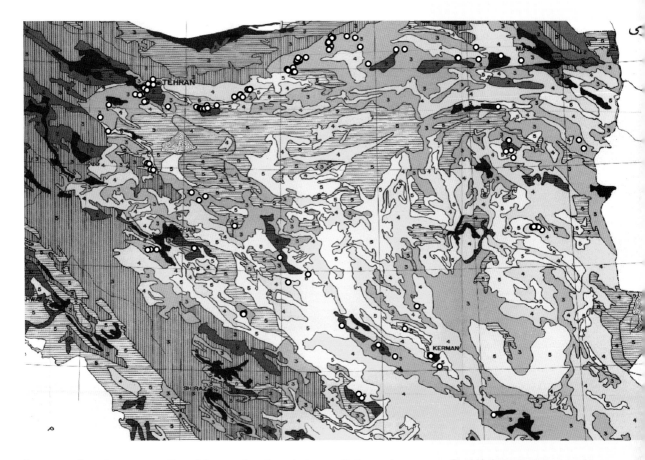

be viewed with caution. In addition, local variations of the soil conditions may blur the general picture. Much more detailed investigations would be required to obtain a clearer picture. The ice house sites of the Project are found near all categories of soils, although apparently with the largest numbers within the zones of reasonable soil potentiality, and with soils which possess a grain size distribution that makes the soil suitable for mud brick fabrication.

The soil map of Iran, Fig. 4.13, lists the prevailing Iranian soils within the project area as follows:[26]

· Type 1: Fine textured alluvial soils, and type 1-4: saline alluvial soils.
· Type 3-4: Salt marsh soils.
· Type 5: Desert soils, often cemented, and types 5-2a/b loose desert soils/sand dunes.
· Types 6, 13, 14, 15, 16: Humus-deficient and calcareous desert soils, locally gypsiferous.

Fig. 4.12. Soil potentiality map of Iran with ice house sites. (Map appended to Dewan and Famouri, 1964)

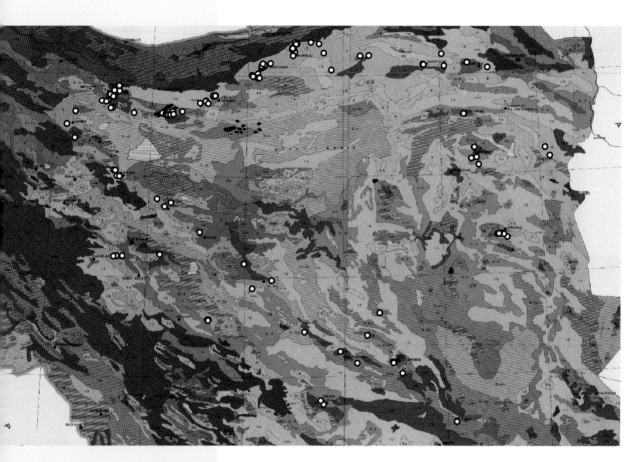

Fig. 4.13. Soil map of Iran with ice house sites. (Map appended to Dewan and Famouri, 1964)

In summary: All ice house sites are situated on alluvial fans and plains of young geological age, where temporary, often violent streams may change the form of the landscape near the mountains. This is less true in the areas of the village ice houses because they are located downstream near oases and orchards, where the alluvial fan slopes have become plains. The village ice houses are all located near agricultural areas of varying quality but always dependant on irrigation. The prevailing soils are:

- Fine textured alluvial soils, often saline: In the areas south of Tehran (at ice house sites YC·9, 10, 11, 12, 13, 14, 15, 16, 17, and 20), around Garmsar (YC·54, 55, 56, 57, 58, 59, 60, 61, 62, 63, 64, and 65), south of Sabzevar (YC·108, 109, 110, and 111), around Nishabur (YC·12 and 113), at Kashmar (YC·115), at Gonabad (YC·120, 121, and 122), at Meybod (YC·34), at Anar (YC·23), Rafsanjan (YC·24), Kabutar Khan (YC·25), in and around Kerman (YC·26, 27, 28, 29, and 30, and in Bam (YC·31).

- Fine textured, calcareous soils, seldom saline: In the areas around Semnan (YC·66, 67, 68, 69, 70, 71, 72, 73, and 74), around Damghan (YC·75, 76, 77, 78, 79, 80, 81, 82, 83, 84, 85, 86, and 87), around Shahrud (YC·88, 89, 90, 91, 92, 93, 94, 95, 96, 97, 98, 99, 100, 101, 102, 103, 104, and 105), around Sir-jan (YC·32 and 33), and Abarqu (YC·37, 38, and 39)

The composition of the soils at the ice house sites themselves was found to be clayey, with contents of silt (loam) and fine sand. At some sites near the mountains, like Kan (YC·7), northwest of Teh-ran, and several Birjand locations (YC·123-128), the clay for the ice house walls contained gravel and stones, almost like a morainal clay, but more plastic. In ASTM (American Society for Testing Materi-als) terminology, the clay used for mud brick and mortar fabrication could be classified as CL, which is described as "inorganic clays of low to medium plasticity, gravelly/sandy/silty/lean clays, with more than 50 weight percent being under 0.075 mm grain size".

Climate

The concentration of ice houses without ice-making in the north along the Elburz Mountains and around Gonabad, and the con-centration of ice houses with ice-making in the western part of the Project Area, on the Sabzevar-Khaf axis, and around Birjand in Khorasan, raise the suspicion that warmer winter temperatures in the north may have made in-situ ice-making difficult. In order to clarify that question the climate data in Fig. 3.2 (on page 31) were split up into two groups - The P-Group comprised of all climate stations at locations with in-situ ice fabrication (32 in all), and the O-Group consisting of the stations at the storage-only ice house sites (8 nos.).

	P	O	Total
No. of days with frost, average per year	65	65	65
No. of days with -4 degrees or less	24	23	23

The average values for the two areas are practically identical and thus indicate that temperature played no role in the fact that ice was not made in-situ at the northern O-sites. In addition, in spite of identical temperature conditions in the western part of the Project Area, and around the towns of Sabzevar, Khaf and Birjand in Khorasan, ice was actually produced in-situ there. So, winter temperatures did not determine when and where ice was fabricated at ice houses. This observation supports the theory that ice was not made on the northern ice house sites because it was simply easier and cheaper to haul the ice from the nearby Elburz Mountains.

The climate data for the Project Area in Fig. 3.2 were established on the basis of information from 1950 to 2005, for the oldest meteorological stations, and for shorter periods from more recent stations. However, if the operation of ice houses in Iran extends back 2,500 years, it seemed important to check whether any significant climate changes have taken place over that period. Researchers at the U.S Environmental Protection Agency (EPA) in a recent study (2008: 3) have assessed that there has been stability in the Earth's climate during the last 2,000 years. Only three minor departures from this stability have taken place in this period: (a) The Medieval Climate Anomaly. Evidence suggests that between 900 and 1300 AD Europe, Greenland and Asia experienced relative warmth; (b) The Little Ice Age. Evidence supports the existence of a colder period between 1500 and 1850 AD, in which temperatures were as much as one degree Celsius less than today, but with local variations; and (c) The Industrial Era. An additional warm period has emerged in the last 100 years, coinciding with substantially increased emissions of greenhouse gases from human activities. Christensen reports that most specialists agree that no significant overall climate changes have occurred over the last millennia. However, local micro-climatic fluctuations happen all the time, often with consequences for agriculture (1993: 11).

Based on these reassurances that major temperature changes have not occurred during the last 2,000 years, the Iranian climate statistics from the period 1950 to 2005 have been used for the analyses of this project without reservations.

Water

During the survey it was extremely difficult to determine the source of the water supply for the ice house sites, i.e. the ice house sites where in-situ ice production had taken place. As has happened with the mud brick buildings, the associated facilities such as qanats, water channels, weirs, settling basins, ponds, etc. were all left to decay and disappear. In addition to the often futile observations in the field, a complete review of the water supply options was undertaken on the 1:500,000 maps – and when available, 1:50,000 maps - for all the sites with a P code, i.e. probable in-situ ice-making. The map review helped to confirm whether qanat water or a motor pump, or in rare cases river or well water, had been at the disposal of the communities. It was important, of course, that the local water was not salty, as this condition would hamper the ice-making process.

The topographical maps suggest that qanats supplied water to the following provinces:

Tehran, Kerman, Yazd, Isfahan (except for the area around the town proper in the Zayandeh River valley), Semnan (including the Garmsar, Semnan, Damghan, and Shahrud sectors), Razavi Khorasan (western part), and South Khorasan. At all these locations traces of the qanat systems were observed.

Motor pumps seemed to have supplied water at the following locations:

Qom Province (Taghrud), Markazi Province (Saveh) and Razavi Khorasan (Nishabur).
The water supply was not clear at Mehdiabad in Markazi Province.

Qanat systems disappear fast. Over the past 50 years, the water supply in the countryside has been taken over by motor pumps. Iran once had had about 40,000 qanats (Tapper, R., and K. McLachlan 2003: 8), however there were only an estimated few thousand left at the time of the survey. These remaining few are dependent on regular maintenance for their continued existence.

I only saw one active qanat at an ice house site, at Zafaranieh in Razavi Khorasan province (YC·111, see photo on book jacket), and an active qanat stream in the village of Mazdj, but only dry channels at the ice house (YC·99). And I saw only one crew of qanat-builders (*moqânni-hâ*) at work – between Sirjan and Shahrbabak – during my 40 days of travelling through the Project Area.

Desert Proximity

The Desert Map in Fig. 4.14 appears of no great value to the ice house project. The original map is of such great scale - 1:2.5 million – that the ice house plots are just pin-pricks on a coarse fabric. However, a few remarks may be appropriate in view of the near-desert location of many of the surveyed ice houses. One major desert region in Iran is the Dasht-e-Kavir, situated within the large triangle formed by the cities of Tehran (in the northwest), Sabzevar (in the east) and Yazd (in the south). This triangle is dominated by large salt lakes and salt swamps. The ice houses are situated far from these unfriendly regions, with only the ice houses of Abbasabad (YC·106), Sadrabad (YC·107), Sabzevar (YC·108, 109, 110) and of the Damghan area (YC·75 to YC·85) close to what the desert map describes as "clay-surfaced desert". This designation is not surprising as these locations are found in the areas rated low in terms of soil quality and potentiality, cf. page 72.

Large sand dune areas – some 20 square kilometers - were sighted east and south of Forat (YC·79) and Hassanabad (YC·80), in the area south of Damghan. (See the photo opposite page 1). However, these areas were not large enough to be included on the desert map.

The other major desert region in Central Iran is the Kavir-e-Lut, situated in south-east Iran within the large triangle formed by Birjand (in the north), Zahedan (in the east), Bam (in the south), and Kerman (in the west). The Kavir-e-Lut is dominated by thousands of square kilometers of sand desert, called "Sandy Hills" on the map. According to the desert map, the Kerman ice houses (YC·26, 27, 28, 29 and 30) are situated close to a smaller sand desert area not sighted during the survey.

As could be expected, the ice houses of Dah Namak (YC·64 and 65) east of Garmsar, Zavareh (YC·46) between Kashan and Na'in, Sirjan, Mahmoudabad and Kabutar Khan (YC·32, 33 and 25) southwest of Kerman, are all situated on or near "clay-surfaced desert" areas, according to the desert map.

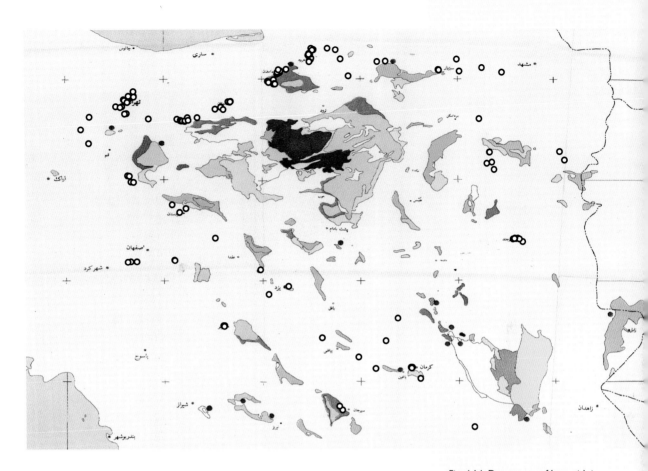

Fig. 4.14. Desert map of Iran with ice house sites (National Geographical Organization, c. 2000)

5 | Domed ice houses - description and analysis

Opposite page
YC-22 Ravar

The description and analyses in this and the following chapter – for obvious reasons - include only the 104 ice houses that were seen to still endure in some form during the survey in the period 2007 to 2009. The description of the ice houses is organized by their shape, their location (village/town or caravansary/fort) and then by the province in which they are situated.

Domed village ice houses - with or without ice plant DVP and DVO types

The domed ice houses located during the survey always served either villages or caravansaries and forts, i.e. they were of the types DV or DC, split into DVP/DVO on one side and DCP/DCO on the other.

The split between identified village ice houses with associated ice-making plant, i.e. shading walls (type DVP), and ice houses with no shading walls (type DVO), is almost 50/50, being 48 DVP types and 51 DVO types. Of the 82 village ice houses still existing in some form, 39 had an ice-making plant (i.e. DVP type) and 43 had none (i.e. DVO type), i.e. the numerical distribution is of the order 50/50 percent for still existing sites (i.e. with remains/ruins) and for the totality of registered sites.

Although some domed ice houses are now situated in towns – like for instance Semnan, Sabzevar, Birjand and Kerman – they were judged to have been clearly outside the towns during their time of operation. Nevertheless, it cannot be excluded that domed ice houses also were used in town areas – possibly in Kashan, where local enquiries indicated that there once had been several ice houses in the present town area. So, despite the V (village) designation assigned during the survey, some of the domed ice houses may also have served the inhabitants of the nearby town. In other words, the use of the code letter V (for village), T (for town) or C (for caravansary) does not imply the only category of clients, only the estimated primary customer category.

It seems significant that all DVO type ice houses, i.e. simple ice storage reservoirs (51, with the exception of one at Mahabad near Kashan), are found along the southern piedmont of the Elburz Mountains on a line from south of Tehran to Nishabur, and around Gonabad in the east (see map in Fig. 5.1). There are only 17 ice houses with an ice making plant (DVP type) in this piedmont zone between Tehran and Nishabur. Surely, it is equally significant that, with the exception of the Mahabad (YC·45) example, only the classical domed ice house type with ice-making plant (DVP) is found in the wide zone south and southeast of the town of Kashan, including Yazd and Kerman Provinces.

The reasons for this particular distribution of chiefly simple "storage only ice houses" in the north, and of almost exclusively classical "storage with ice-making ice houses" in the highlands between the large deserts and the Zagros Mountains are not immediately clear. But a reasonable explanation is that because the "storage only ice houses" in the north were located so near to the Elburz Mountains it would have been easier and cheaper for the ice house owners to have transported ice from the mountains to the domed storage facilities, rather than to have made ice themselves on site, involving the procurement of fresh water, waiting for frosty nights, as well as requiring a lot of work for both building and operation. In addition, the quality of "mountain ice" was invariably higher than that of ice produced in basins or ponds dug out of the sandy clay subsoil.

On the other hand, in the west and in the east the high mountains were mostly at a great distance from the ice houses, and it would have been more feasible to build a local facility for ice-making, like for instance in Abarqu. It would then have been a condition that such localities would have had sufficient water. These aspects will be analyzed in some detail later.

The map in Fig. 5.1. shows the situation of the domed village ice houses, which constitute the majority of all recorded ice houses, in total 99 nos. The map illustrates well one of the main discoveries of the study: It shows clearly the predominance of ice houses without an ice-making plant (DVO type) in the north, along the south side

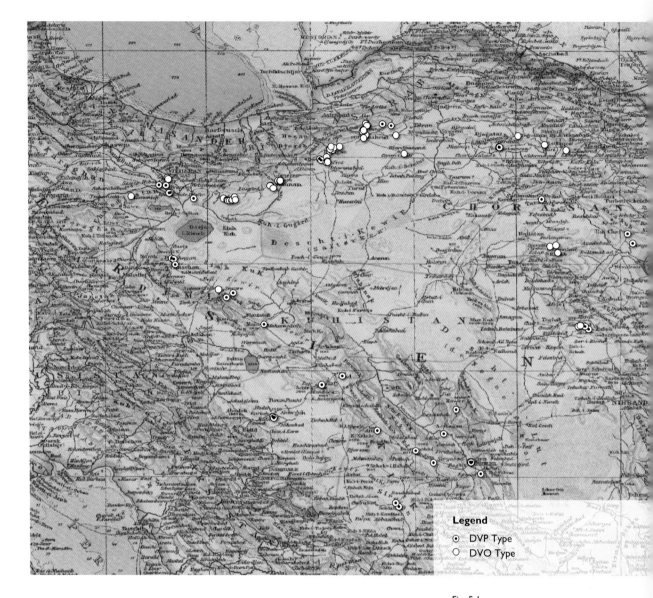

Legend
⊙ DVP Type
○ DVO Type

of the Elburz Mountains, and the predominance of ice houses with ice-making plant (DVP) in the wide band on the east side of the Zagros Mountains.

The following abbreviations and terms are used in the detailed ice house descriptions which follow in this chapter:

YC: Ice House ID number
H: Assessed height, meters
D: Assessed external diameter, meters
Gradient: Average slope of dome surface, degrees
V: Assessed ice pit volume, m^3

Fig. 5.1.
Locations of domed village ice houses
DVP and DVO types

Fig. 5.2. YC·11 Aliabad
View from northwest
Water melon field and irrigation
channel in foreground

Details can be found in the Ice House Catalogue of my dissertation, which contains all directly registered data and all photographs for the ice houses surveyed under this project. Such information is available on request from the author.

Tehran Province

Domed ice houses with ice plant
DVP type

YC·11 Aliabad
H/D: 14/17 m. Dome shape: Rounded cone/paraboloid. Gradient: 70 degrees. V: Approx. 600 m³.

No access to the inside of the ice house was possible. The dome had apparently been restored and plastered to form a smooth surface. The vent at the top had been plugged. The dome was situated on a closed-off property, apparently private, which is surprising in view of the ice house's official registration. Shading walls (100 m long) are crumbling; there are 10 m long wing walls at either end as can be seen in Figures 5.2 and 5.3.

YC·12 Hakimabad
H/D: 15/22 m. Dome shape: Rounded cone/paraboloid. Gradient: 45 degrees. V: 1000 m³.

This is the largest ice house in the northwest part of the Project Area. The wall thickness at terrain level is as much as 3 meters in order to support the dome with an average gradient of only 45 degrees (i.e. on average 1:1 slope). The ice house is crumbling, inside and outside, where the footway spiraling to the top is an obvious weak area for rain and wind erosion. The outer surface of the dome and the 100 m long shading wall are slowly melting away.

YC·13 Robat Karim
H/D: 9/14 m; measurements are rough estimates as the ice house was very worn and damaged. The gradient was assumed once to have been of the order of 60 degrees. V: Approx. 600 m³.

The ice pit is almost filled up with collapsed and melted dome clay material. The remains of two parallel east-west running shading walls are visible, but they are disappearing rapidly. The photograph in Fig. 5.4 indicates a configuration similar to YC·38, Abarqu I (Fig. 1.2), i.e. a domed ice house with two or three shading walls towards the west.

YC·17 Koleyn
H/D: 11/16 m. Dome shape: Cone with two steps each of four meter's height. Gradient: 45 degrees. Fig 5.5 and Fig 5.6.

Fig. 5.3. YC·11 Aliabad
Aerial view from Google Earth

Fig. 5.4. YC·13 Robat Karim
View from west

Fig. 5.5. YC·17 Koleyn
View from west

Fig. 5.6. YC·17 Koleyn
Aerial view from Google Earth

The dome, outside and inside, had been restored and repaired, but was locked-off. A heap of *kâh-gel* (mud-straw) mortar on the site indicated occasional repair activity. The sixty meter shading wall on the west side was in moderate decay. Local people reported that there once was one more ice house- now demolished - in the area between Koleyn and Hassanabad, possibly at a location called Arad.

Domed ice houses without ice plant
DVO type

YC·10 Tarshanbeh
H/D: 12/16 m. Dome shape: Rounded cone/paraboloid. Gradient: 55 degrees. V: 350 m³.

The outside surface of the dome is completely restored and plastered to a smooth surface, and the top vent is plugged. The ice pit and pit ledge were restored by means of baked brick masonry. Neighboring walls were found close-by on two sides of the dome. Photographs and drawings of the Tarshanbeh ice house can be found in the Robat Karim Museum, probably prepared by the *Sâzmân-e-Mirâs Farhangi* organization.[27] There is an obvious discrepancy between the shape and dimensions of the ice house on the photos and on the drawings at the museum. The same problem has been observed on several MF drawings from other sites.

General comments on the domed ice houses · Tehran Province

It seemed during inspection that all the ice house domes in Tehran Province once had had ventilation holes at the top, but that such vents had been plugged on those domes that had been restored. The outer surfaces of the domes were either smoothly plastered (YC·10-11-12) or stepped (YC·17). YC·13, at Robat Karim, was too decayed for an assessment.

All domes had visible mud brick shells inside; only the Hakimabad dome had a decorative course of bricks turned 45 degrees around their vertical axis. This decorative layer was situated five meters from the top of the dome. All mud brick courses were horizontal, with successive courses corbelled to create a narrowing of the rings of mud brick courses towards the top of the dome. The average H/D ratio for the domes was 74%, with a large variation of side angles (68-82%), i.e. no two are exactly alike. The dome foundations could not be inspected, but probably consisted of simple *kâh-gel/piseh* (straw-mud) material, or *sefteh*, i.e. *kâh-gel/piseh* with stone ballast. These materials are described in detail later in this book.

All ice house domes had doors, most often at the eastern and western sides. At Koleyn, inside the dome, there was a narrow pit-ledge from where ladders would lead into the ice pit (and up from it). There were no fixed staircases observed in the pits, except at the re-built ice pit of Tarshanbeh. Only a few of the ice pits were accessible for inspection. The Tarshanbeh and Koleyn ice house pits had been restored by means of baked and mud bricks, respectively, while Hakimabad and Robat Karim had simple, unlined ice pits dug out of the natural subsoil. Shading walls were all built up of *kâh-gel* courses, locally reinforced by mud bricks. No focused restoration of these walls had taken place.

None of the ice house complexes had any trace of ice ponds or water channels for ice-making. The water would have come from qanats or, more probably, from wells (*motor*) in the area.

No indications of time of construction could be determined during the survey. The National Register attributes the construction of the ice house at Tarshanbeh to the Safavid Period (1491-1722) and of the Aliabad ice house to the Qadjar Period (1796-1925). However, the frequency and extent of restoration and rebuilding of the two ice houses are unknown.

During the survey there was a distinct sense that many more domed ice houses had once existed in the southern vicinity of Tehran, as it was reported to me by local sources during visits to completely cleared sites in Shahr Rey (at the Shah Abdol Azim mosque complex and elsewhere), Varamin (at the location Hezar Zurgh), and Arad near Hassanabad.

Markazi Province

Domed ice houses with ice plant
DVP type

None found.

Domed ice houses with no ice plant
DVO type

YC·20 Mehdiabad
H/D: 9/13 m. Dome shape: The cone was recently restored with steps of 0.5 meters to facilitate repair.
Gradient: 55 degrees (H/D = 0.7)

The interior of the ice house had been restored and converted into an amphitheatre style space at ground level with a large door on the north side (Fig. 5.7). There was a 20 cm-wide vent at the top of the dome. This ice house is situated in the middle of an open plain, and no ice-making plant was visible at this location. It is located in that part of Markazi Province that protrudes into the Project Area, about 50 kilometers north of Saveh, in the direction of Tehran. According to the National Register, this ice house is of Qadjar era origin.

Fig. 5.8 YC·21 Ravar
View from east

Kerman Province

Domed ice houses with ice plant
DVP type

YC·21 Ravar

H/D: 11/16 m. Dome shape: The recently restored cone had 0.5 meter steps for easy access. Gradient: 45 degrees. V: 600 m³.

The dome surface and shading walls were nicely repaired and plastered with *kâh-gel* mortar. There was a small vent at the top of the dome. The area north of the ice house and the shade wall had been converted into a public park and playground, with a public toilet in the shape of a small ice house. No trace existed of ice ponds and the water supply system. The ice house is in the National Registry and there noted to be of Qadjar origin.

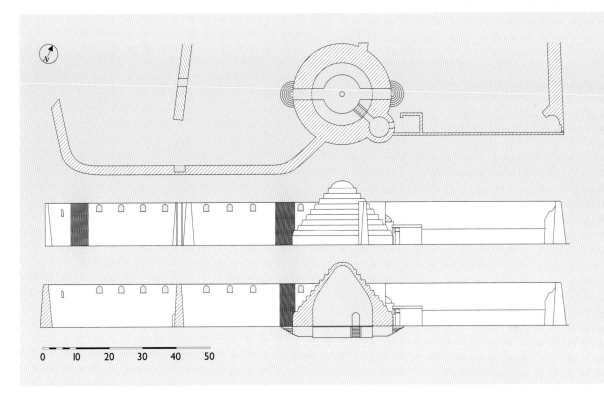

Fig. 5.9 YC·21 Ravar
Layout and cross section

YC·23 Anar

H/D: 13/14 m – dimensions are estimated, as the ice house was much damaged. Gradient: 60 degrees. V: 400 m³.

The dome shape was a rounded cone. There were traces inside the dome of one course of wood inserts at about 8 meters height. All surfaces were deteriorating fast, including the two 30 meter-shading walls on either side of the dome (Fig. 5.10). This crumbling ice house was situated outside town and received no attention in spite of an official registration. The National Registration data could not be obtained because the pertaining page in my copy of the official book was missing

YC·24 Hadj Ali Agha at Abassabad/Rafsanjan

H/D: 12/16 m. The dome shape was a cone. Gradient: 45 degrees; the outer surface of the dome was made as 0.7-meter (restored) recessed steps for easy access. V: 500 m³.

There was once probably a small vent at the top of the dome. The ice pit had been carefully restored with a plain earth floor, but Hourcade reports that there originally was a drain at the bottom of the pit for the collection of melt water (1994: 92). The shading wall

Fig. 5.10. YC·23 Anar
Classical DVP type, view from east

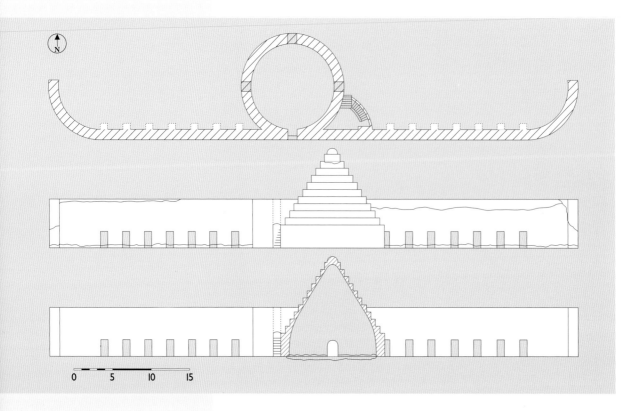

Fig. 5.11. YC·23 Anar
Layout and cross section

(toward the west of the dome) has been nicely rebuilt and restored, while all traces of water basins and channels were removed when the area was converted into a public park. The age of the original installation is reported by the cultural authorities to be of late Qadjar origin (1920 AD).

YC·25 Kabutar Khan

H/D: 13/13 m. Dome shape: A restored paraboloid with twelve 0.4-meter steps, sitting on a 3 meter high plinth (a truncated cone). Gradient: 60 degrees. V: 400 m³. Fig 5.12.

This design is similar to the Moayedi and Zarisf ice houses in Kerman (YC·26 and 28), see below. Shading walls were crumbling.

YC·26 Moayeri/Kerman

H/D: 15/21 m. Dome shape: Parabola with twelve 0.7-meter successively receding steps, sitting on a six meter high plinth. Gradient: 55 degrees. V: 600 m³. Fig. 5.13 and Fig. 5.14.

This installation is judged by the cultural authorities to be of Safavid origin, i.e. from earlier than 1790 AD. There have been great improvements made to this ice house from the pathetic structure I

Fig. 5.12. YC·25 Kabutar Khan
View from east

Fig. 5.13. YC·26 Moayeri
View from east

first visited outside town in 1966.[28] The dome and the ornamented shading walls were carefully restored in the early 1980s and plastered with *kâh-gel*. The floor and seating ranks of the ice house had been converted into a moquette-clad amphitheatre auditorium cum office of a youth organization. The vent at the top of the dome, diameter about 70 centimeters, still existed and might allow the occasional rain to hit the computers on the ice pit floor. The entire area around the ice house and the shading walls has been converted into a public park and playground.

In the early 1970's, Stevens included the Moayedi ice house on his map of Kerman, at a distance of one kilometer from the Friday Mosque near the city center, but with no description (1974: 70). The Kerman Moayedi ice house is one of the three ice houses usually

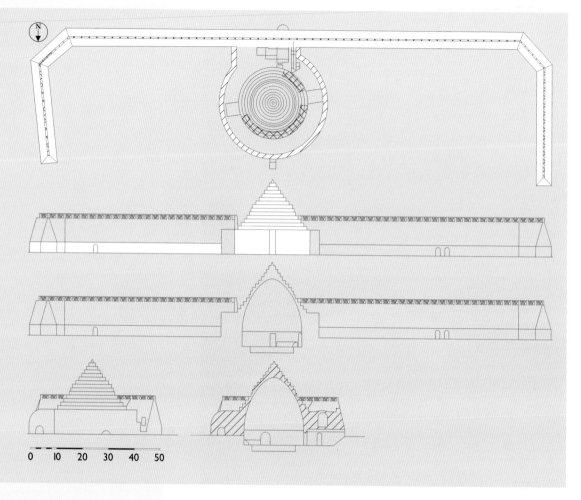

Fig. 5.14. YC·26 Moayeri
Layout and cross section

Fig. 5.15. YC·27 Rigabad
Aerial view from Google Earth

mentioned in the tourist guide books for Iran. The other two are the ice houses at Meybod and Abarqu in Yazd Province (see later).

YC·27 Rigabad/Kerman

H/D: 13/21 m. The dome shape is a paraboloid with twelve successively receding 0.8-meter steps, sitting on a three meter high plinth. Gradient: 45 degrees.

The ice house was locked off. The dome and the ornamented shading wall to the west had been restored. Old aerial photographs showed that there had been a second, long curved shading wall, symmetrically situated towards the east (Rainer 1977: 198). This eastern wall had been completely demolished and removed to make room for a large boulevard next to the ice house. See the photographs in Fig. 8.4 and Fig. 8.5. and a complete description in chapter 8 on page 204.

YC·28 Zarisf/Kerman

H/D 16/22 m. The dome shape is a paraboloid, with fifteen 0.8-meter successively receding steps, on a four meter high plinth. Gradient: 65 degrees. Fig. 5.16 and Fig. 5.18.

The ice house was locked off. The ice house and the ornamented shading walls were in the (slow) process of restoration. Between my two visits in August 2007 and February 2008 new damage to the plinth surface had occurred. There seemed to be a watchman residing at this site, but he was not sighted during the visits.

YC·29 Djo Moyedi/Kerman

This ice house of presumed Qadjar era origin was included in the National Registry (Pazooki, N., and A. Shadmehr 2005: 334), but not included in the list of Kerman Province ice houses given to me by the local *Mirâs Farhangi* office at a visit in February 2008. It is believed to have disappeared.

YC·30 Langar/Mahan

H/D 13/16 m. The original dome shape is unclear due to decay, but it is probably a stepped paraboloid on a two meter plinth base. Gradient: 55 degrees. V: 500 m³. Fig. 5.17.

It is reported to be of Qadjar era origin.

YC·32 Sirjan

This ice house has two domes connected by 110 meter long, curved shading walls. H/D: 10/13 m for both domes. The dome shape is a slightly curved dome cone with thirteen 0.7 meter steps on a one meter plinth base. Gradient: 57 to 47 degrees. V is estimated at 2 x 350 m³ (no access to pits). Fig. 5.19 and Fig. 5.20.

The domes and the decorated walls are nicely restored; the surrounding area has been made into a public park and playground.

YC·33 Mahmoudabad

H/D: 12/16 m. The original dome shape is unclear due to decay, but it was probably a stepped parabola. Gradient: 60 degrees. V: 600 m³.

The satellite image indicates that there once was a shading wall toward the west; only an almost completely melted section remains near the ice house dome.

Fig. 5.16. YC·28 Zarisf
View from south

Fig. 5.17. YC·30 Langar/Mahan
View from north-east

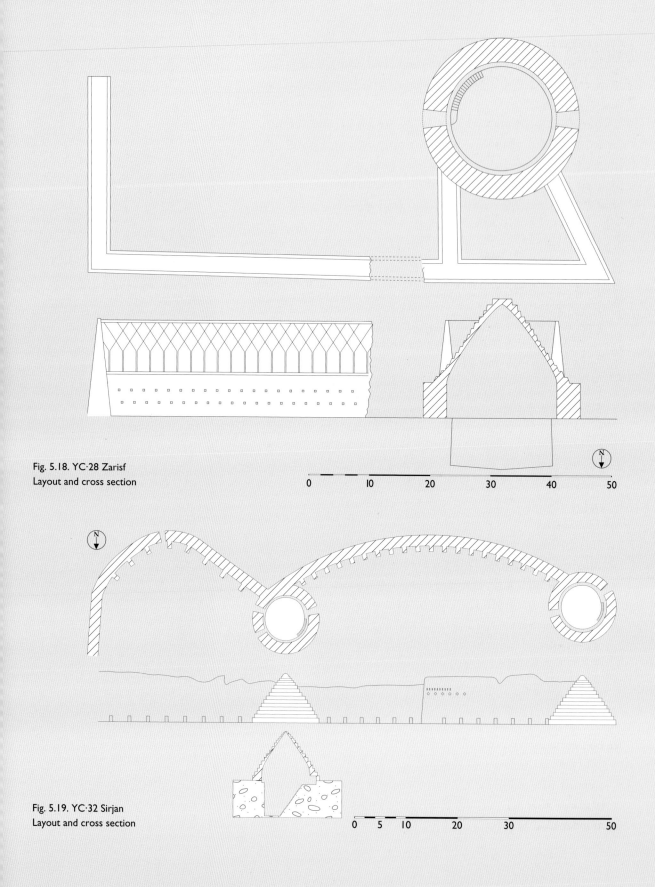

Fig. 5.18. YC·28 Zarisf
Layout and cross section

0   10   20   30   40   50

Fig. 5.19. YC·32 Sirjan
Layout and cross section

0   5   10   20   30   50

Domed ice houses with no ice plant
DVO type

Fig. 5.20. YC·32 Sirjan
Twin domes and shading walls

There were no simple ice storage houses (i.e. without shading walls) located in the province of Kerman. The reason could be one, or a combination, of the following:

· There are no nearby high mountains to deliver natural ice, so in-situ ice production was necessary.
· There is an abundant water supply available due to the many qanats, which made in-situ ice-making a favored option in view of the many frost-days per year and the high altitude of the sites.

General comments · Kerman Province

Ice house shapes in Kerman Province fell into two categories:

· Stepped parabolids/cones with gradients of 45 to 60 degrees (Ravar, Rafsanjan, and supposedly at Anar, Langar and Mahmoudabad).

- Stepped paraboloids on plinths of heights between one and six meters (Sirjan, Rigabad, Kabutar Khan and Moayedi).

The average H/D ratio for domes without a plinth base was 78 percent, with only the example at Anar having a more pointed shape than the others. The existence of a plinth under the dome reduced the average H/D to the order of 70 to 75 percent. Some similarity of design was noted for the domes with plinths but the sizes varied greatly. The dome of the ice house at Anar (YC·23) may be seen as a typical example of a frequently occurring mixture of a cone and a parabola. The original outside height and diameter of the dome was assessed at 12 and 16 meters, respectively, a size that is matched at several locations in Kerman Province (YC·21 Ravar, YC·24 Abassabad/Rafsanjan, YC·30 Langar/Mahan, and YC·33 Mahmoudabad/Sirjan). All domes probably once had vents at the top, but at Rafsanjan, Kabutar Khan, Rigabad and Sirjan they had been plugged in connection with their restoration.

Doors in the domes were usually placed at the east and west sides, at Anar also at the north side. All domes accessed had visible mud bricks inside; at Anar there was a mud brick course with a row of holes which had accommodated wood inserts. Dome foundations could not be inspected, but the material seemed to be simple *kâh-gel* lifts at Ravar, Anar and Mahmoudabad. Where ice pits could be inspected, their wall material was natural subsoil; only Mahmoudabad had a stone wall lined ice pit.

At the well restored ice houses at Ravar, Rafsanjan, Moayedi, Rigabad, Zarisf and Sirjan, the restoration had included the shading walls, the upper meter of which had ornamented parapets, and, at Zarisf, large mud brick ornaments on the sides.

There were no traces of a water supply system at any of the ice houses, which were presumably fed by the several qanats in the area, or by motor pumps. Incidentally, a village near Langar/Mahan was called Qanatestan, i.e. "qanat land".

As regards the age of the ice houses, no indications were found on the sites proper, and the recent repairs and renovations had concealed possible traces. However, the National Register (Pazooki, N., and A. Shadmehr 2005) indicates the following:

- Ravar, Abassabad/Rafsanjan, Djo Moyedi, Zarisf, Langar and Sirjan: Qadjar period (1796-1925 AD);

Fig. 5.21. YC·38 Abarqu II
View from west

Yazd Province

Domed village ice houses with ice-making plant
DVP type

YC·37 Abarqu I

H/D: 18/20.5 m. The dome was an almost (reverse) funnel shape with a 55 degree steep conical main body, with sixteen recessed steps at 0.8 meters. V: 1000 m³.

The ice house dome had been recently restored but showed already some damage at the top. The three parallel shading walls on the west side had received no attention at all and were crumbling. There are, however, faint traces of the ice ponds that were once in operation on the north side of the shade walls. This ice house has become a tourist attraction because it is located within sight of the Abarqu Tourist Inn, where many tourists make a stopover between Shiraz and Yazd. A plaque in front of the ice house states that the ice house is of Safavid origin, while the Yazd Culture Magazine (2004) dates it to the Qadjar Period. Refer to the photograph of this ice house in Fig. 1.2. for a current view. An old photograph from 1970 is shown in Fig. 5.23 on page 102.

Fig. 5.22. YC·39 Abarqu III
View from east

YC·38 Abarqu II

H/D: 17/20 m. The dome shape was almost a cone with an angle of 65 degrees. V: 1100 m³. Fig. 5.21.

The outer surface was smooth, with a staircase spiraling to the top vent on the east side. The dome appears to have had some repair done to its outer surface in recent years, while the inside surface and the three crumbling shading walls have received no attention at all. Local contacts explained that this ice house had been supplied with water from a qanat, which surfaced at Faraqeh, 25 kilometers to the west, from where an open stream (*Nakh-e-Biyâbân*) took the water to the agricultural area at which the ice house was located. Today, there is no trace of the earlier fertile area and the water supply works. The photograph in Fig. 5.21 gives a good impression of how the shading walls were built, mainly of *kah-gel* lifts, but locally strengthened by mud bricks. And it is seen that no maintenance of the mud structure leads to great vulnerability to heavy rains as they may occur.

YC·39 Abarqu III (or Hek)

H/D: 18/22 m. Dome shape: Almost conical with an angle of 69 degrees, on top of a three-meter base. V: 1000 m³. Fig. 5.22.

As at Abarqu II, this ice house appeared to have received some cosmetic treatment of the outer stepped dome surface, but none inside or at the three disintegrating shading walls.

Domed village ice houses with no ice plant
DVO type

No ice houses without an ice plant were found in Yazd Province, presumably for reasons similar to those already stated for Kerman Province, i.e. ice-bearing mountains are too far away, and favorable water and frost conditions exist for ice-making in winter.

General comments · Yazd Province

Together with the Meybod ice house (classified as DCP - caravan ice house, see later, because of its association with the Meybod Road Station), the three Abarqu ice houses are the largest in Iran, in terms of the size of their domes. They are all 18-19 meters tall and have diameters of 20 to 23 meters. In addition, all three domes had large open vents at the top, with diameters from 0.8 to 1.0 meters.

In spite of their almost identical main dimensions they represent three different designs:

· Abarqu I is reverse funnel-shaped at 55 degrees slope, with one meter recessed steps and with mud brick knobs distributed over the surface for maintenance access (ref. Fig. 1.2).
· Abarqu II is almost cone shaped at 65 degrees slope, with a smooth plastered surface and a staircase winding to the top for access without a scaffold (ref. Fig. 5.21).
· Abarqu III is similarly almost cone shaped, but at 69 degrees slope and with large 1.5 meter receding steps. Fig. 5.22.

All three domes had received restoration and some maintenance. Figure 5.23 shows the Abarqu I ice house photographed by Beazley in 1970 which can be compared to the photograph taken by me

Fig. 5.23. YC·37 Abarqu I in 1970 (Beazley, E., and M. Harverson 1982: 54). Same ice house as in Fig. 1.2.

in 2007 (Fig. 1.2). Apart from the evident restoration of the dome that has taken place since 1970, it is clear that the shading walls in the foreground have received no treatment. I could faintly distinguish the former ice ponds along the crumbling walls at all three complexes, but there is no trace of the water supply system. At the time of ice house operation, water was brought into Abarqu via a 30 kilometer open channel (*Nakh-e-Biyâbân*, later piped) from the village of Faraqeh, where a 10 kilometer long qanat from the western mountains emerged. In 1955 the ground water table at Abarqu was 30 meters below the surface; in 2008 the depth was 200 meters, which is a good indication of what modern pumps and uncontrolled exploitation have inflicted on the environment, including the water resources.

The Abarqu ice houses displayed original reinforcements of the inner mud brick shell, either by the insertion of single courses of baked bricks (Abarqu I and II), or two layers of wooden inserts (Abarqu III), and the use of stronger mortar and a stone wall at the lower elevation (Abarqu II). The ice pits had been dug into the natural soil; at Abarqu III, the pit was reinforced by stone walls, fragments of which were seen. At all three ice houses the ice pits were in a miserable state, most especially at Abarqu II and III.

Fig. 5.24. YC·40 Mazreh Drum
North entrance

As regards to age, the National Register indicates a Qadjar era origin (1792-1925 AD) for all three Abarqu ice houses.

Attempts were made to find and survey the NR-registered ice houses at Fathabad and Benderabad in Yazd Province, but with no luck in spite of many questions asked. The former ice houses of Yazd and Taft are mentioned in the Ice House List of this project and their existence was confirmed by Ghobadian (1994) and Beazley (photo in Beazley et al. 1982: 56). The Yazd ice house had been demolished by a local entrepreneur "for economic reasons" (Ghobadian 1994: 326), i.e. he wanted to put a modern building in its place. The Taft ice house had simply disappeared; nobovdy could be found who could say what had happened.

Isfahan Province

Domed ice houses with ice plant
DVP type

_____

YC·40 Mazreh Drum[29]

H/D: 13/16 m (the measures are very approximate as the dome is heavily damaged). V: 500 m³. Fig. 5.24.

Even though the dome was partially gone, it was still possible to see three decorative courses of mud bricks turned 45 degrees in the inner shell. The ice house complex includes some auxiliary mud brick buildings nearby, and a 160 meter-long shading wall, all much damaged. Stings by vicious wasps in one of the half-buried mud brick buildings almost ended my odyssey in the Iranian desert.

Fig. 5.25. YC·45 Mahabad
View from southwest

YC·46 Zavareh

H/D: 11/12 m. The dome shape was a pointed and curved cone, with an angle at the base of 70 degrees, placed on a three-meter plinth.

External restoration seemed underway at the time of the visit (2007) as the plinth had been partially re-plastered, and the dome surface was in the process of receiving a new stepped outer shell of mud bricks, later to be plastered. The ice pit was locked off, but the original ice pit volume was estimated at 300 m³. Of the shading wall(s) only a crumbling fraction remained.

YC·53 Nain

H/D: 12/15. Dome shape: Paraboloid, with an average gradient of 60 degrees.

The ice house was situated in a locked-off compound and was only inspected from a helpful neighbor's roof. The ice house and associated walls were in a state of rapid decay.

Domed ice houses with no ice plant
DVO type

YC·45 Mahabad

H/D: 17/22 m. (the dimensions are very approximate, as the dome was heavily damaged, Fig. 5.25).

The ice house site was situated within an enclosure and a close-up examination was not possible. The original side gradient was estimated at 65 degrees. The dome of the ice house seemed to have been as large as the Abarqu ice houses, but had no shading walls. It was situated in a private garden at the thriving agricultural village of Mahabad. The south side of the dome had collapsed, and the still standing residual shell demonstrated the strength of a mud brick dome – even as it was subjected to great local tension forces. Nevertheless, it is simply a question of time before the dome collapses and disappears entirely.

General comments · Isfahan Province.

The domed ice houses of Isfahan province were all situated on the western fringe of the Dasht-e-Kavir desert on an almost straight line from Kashan to Nain. They were of varying design, with smooth side slopes between 60 and 70 degrees, and all presumed to have had vents at the top, although it was not always possible to verify this. In addition, the inner mud brick surfaces varied: For instance, at Mazreh Drum, the lower part of the inner wall was plastered with mud paste. Only at Zavareh was a restoration effort underway. The Zavareh ice house had east and west doors. Foundations could not be inspected at any site.

The shading walls at Zavareh and Nain had been partly demolished. No trace was found of ice ponds and water supply systems, but qanats, and later motor pumps, had fed the ice plants in the area.

The National Register dates the ice house at Mazreh Drum to the Safavid Period, and the example at Nain to the Qadjar Period. Despite their NR registration, both ice houses were rapidly deteriorating.

Fig. 5.26. YC·75 Firouzabad
Unlined ice pit wall, drain in bottom
of pit

Semnan Province

Domed ice houses with ice plant
DVP type

YC·67 Sarkheh
The fate of the domed ice house, which allegedly was part of this site, could not be determined; only a section of a shading wall remained at the time of the visit.

YC·68 Sarkheh I
The domed ice houses pictured in MF records may be situated in Sarkheh village at the position 35 27.7N/53 12.6E. It was too late in the work process to return to the area for a visit.

YC·75 Firouzabad
H/D: 15/20 m. V: 1500 m³.

This ice house appears once to have been a masterpiece, both out-side and inside. The outer surface of the cone had 25 very regular steps of 0.6 meters, constructed of mud bricks and mortar. The in-side shell was a largely homogeneous mud brick surface, only pen-etrated by a ring of wood stumps in the brick layer at a height of about four meters. The ice pit (Fig. 5.26) had clearly been excavated in the shape of a reversed truncated cone. It was un-lined, i.e. no wall slope protection, and it had a drain hole at the bottom for pos-sible melt water, making it one of only two observed ice houses that had a drain in the bottom of the ice pit.

The ice house was built in1940-45 by the grandfather of Mrs. Shahla F, whom I met during my visit to Damghan in June 2009. She explained that her grandfather owned the entire village, includ-ing the ice house.

Fig. 5.27. YC·76 Abdolabad
Aerial view from Google Earth

YC·76 Abdolabad

This ice house was not visited, but it appears from the Google Earth imagery to be very similar to Firouzabad above, although smaller. H/D: 12/15 m. V: 900 m³. Fig. 5.27.

YC·90 Saadabad

H/D was 8/9 m, maybe 10/12 m (It was difficult to judge due to the lack of access and view of its lower section).

The design is a conical dome, rounded at the top, and with al-most two meter recessed steps, much eroded. The gradient was 61 degrees. Present use is presumably as a store house. The shading walls could not be accessed.

YC·98 Jilan

Due to the flooding (by qanat water) of the western access road from Mazj at the time of the survey, this site could not be visited. Its approximate position was taken from Google Earth, but no techni-cal data could be obtained.

YC·99 Mazj

The design was a stepped, pointed paraboloid, with an H/D of 12/18 meters. Gradient was 68 degrees, V: 1000 m³.

The associated 40 meters long shading wall was situated to the west of the dome. There were open, and dry, qanat water channels passing the site.

Fig. 5.28. YC·103 Bostam
View from south

Fig. 5.29. YC·103 Bostam
Layout and cross section

YC·102 Hawa'i

At this site, near Bostam, only a huge east-west shading wall, 150 meters long, remained. My local guides explained that earlier there had been a large dome over a 20 meters (?) deep ice pit.

YC·103. Bostam

H/D: 13/16 m. The dome design was a cone, curved at the top. V: 1000 m³. Fig. 5. 28 and Fig. 5.29.

There were wooden struts at irregular intervals spread over the dome surface. The ruin of an attendants' hut was found at the north side.

Domed ice houses with no ice plant
DVO type

YC·55 and YC·56 Ghatul Bozorg and Ghatul Kuchek

The two ice houses were of similar design, situated 100 meters from each other; the larger (Bozorg) with an H/D of 13/20 m, and the smaller with an H/D of 7/9 m. The larger ice house had twenty recessed steps of 0.7 meters, the smaller had thirteen steps of 0.45 meters on a 1.5 meter plinth structure. Gradients at both structures were 55 degrees. V: 1200 and 200 m³, respectively. Fig. 5.30.

Fig. 5.30. YC·55 Ghatul Bozorg
View from north

A stream at the site carried water during the May 2009 visit, although it may dry up in summer. There had been no ice-making on this site.

YC·57 Rikan

The ice house had a design similar to the Ghatul ice houses above. H/D: 8/13 m. Gradient was 55 degrees. V: 800 m³.

The northern half of the dome had been removed to make space for the construction of a roadside building (shop?). The ice house was connected to a farmhouse on the south side, and the farmer's wife asked for help to stop the demolition of her homestead. The local guide explained that the ice pit had been 20 meters deep, which cannot be true; it was probably six, maximum eight meters in depth. The cross section of the wall in Fig. 5.31. illustrates the construction of an ice house dome wall, with three consecutive layers of mud brick walling and plaster on the outside. Remnants of the attached shading wall can be see in the distance.

YC·59 Shah Sefid

The design was similar to that of Ghatul Kuchek (YC·55). H/D: 9/12 m. Gradient: 55 degrees. V: 300 m³.

The ice house had begun to crumble.

Fig. 5.31. YC·57 Rikan
Partly demolished to make space for a road-side shop

Fig. 5.32. YC·60 Sudaghlan
View from south

Fig. 5.33. YC·61 Yahteri
View from east

YC·60 Sudaghlan
The design was similar to that of Ghahtul Kuchek (YC#55). H/D: 6/8 m. Gradient: 55 degrees. V: 150 m³. Fig. 5.32.
The ice house was severely damaged.

YC·61 Yahteri
The cone design was similar to that of Sudaghlan, but the cone was larger, and with a sort of chimney with a cowl on the top vent. H/D: 9/12 m. Gradient: 65 degrees. V: 300 m³. Fig. 5.33.
The ice house was crumbling but still in use as a storage chamber for a nearby dwelling.

YC·62 Padeh
The paraboloid/beehive-shaped dome had an H/D of 11/15 m. The gradient ranged from 65 degrees at ground level to 40 degrees towards the top. V: 500 m³.
Entrance to the dome was locked off.

YC·63 Imamzadeh Zoalefqar
This ice house resembled that at Sudaghlan (YC·60), although less than half the dome was still standing. H/D: 7/9 m.
V: 150 m³.

YC·68 Sarkheh I
Only late in the course of the survey was attention drawn to this ice house and there was no opportunity for a visit. It is believed to be the Sarkheh ice house included in the National Register (NR No. S273).

YC·69 Biabanak
This ice house was located 9 kilometers south of Sarkheh. Its name was found in the *Mirâs Farhangi* (MF) Semnan note on ice houses, although it was too late for a visit.

YC·70 Zaveghan
A pointed, paraboloid design with the outer stepped surface severely eroded and almost gone. H/D: 10/15 m, with 55 degrees gradient. V: 400 m³. Fig. 5.34.
There was a small attendant's hut at the northeast side. The former ventilation hole at the top was covered and plugged. The mud/clay material contains distinct gravel and stone fractions.

Fig. 5.34. YC·70 Zaveghan
View from north

YC·71 Shah Djugh Kuchek

A drawing of this relatively small ice house is included in the Ice House Catalogue; it was obtained from an MF appraisal note. However, the ice house itself could not be found and had presumably been demolished. A check on Google Earth imagery showed no trace. The size had been 4.5/7 meters, and the presumed ice pit volume less than 30 m³.

YC·72 Shah Djugh Bozorg

In spite of a thorough search in the field, this ice house could only be located at a later time on Google Earth imagery. Measurements were taken from an MF appraisal note, which included plan and section. It has a pointed cone with an H/D of 10/16 m, with an external, eroded stepped construction. V: 500 m³. My redrawing of the large Shah Djugh ice house is seen in Fig. 5.35.

YC·73 Ateshgah

This fast crumbling ice house was located within a locked-off private property. It is assumed to have been of a shape similar to that at Shah Djugh Bozorg. H/D had been about 10/13 m. V: 500 m³.

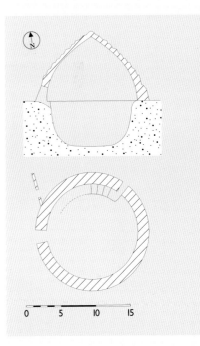

Fig. 5.35 YC·72 Shah Djugh Bozorg
Layout and cross section

Fig. 5.36. YC·74 Mahaleh Chup

Fig. 5.37. YC·77 Alyan
Dome interior, north door

YC·74 Maheleh Chup

This ice house was nearing total destruction, but its pit and lower dome shell were still used as a goat stable (Fig. 5.36). H/D: 12/16 m. V: 700 m³. The remaining top twenty inner mud brick layers are turned slightly and constitute a decorative stepped cone surface.

YC·77 Alyan

The ice house had a large hole at the top and was crumbling, but it was still surprisingly cool inside on a hot summer's day (June 2009). H/D: 13/16 m. V: 800 m³. Fig. 5.37.

The dome was conical with a gradient of 58 degrees. The dome foundation was a classical "*sefteh and kâh-gel*" wall to a height of one meter above ground level.

YC·78 Mohamad-Abadu

The ice house was nearing total destruction, but had probably had an H/D ratio of 9/12. V: 300 m³. Fig. 5.38.

There were qanat shafts around the area where ice may have been produced in open ponds without shading walls.

Fig. 5.39. YC·80 Hassanabad
View from northwest

YC·79 Forat

The conical, stepped ice house was deteriorating, but was still used for storage by the farmer in whose gardens it stands. A window had been added on the north cone side. H/D: 13/16 m. V: 600 m³.

YC·80 Hassanabad

The ice house was standing in the middle of an open field; a cemetery had developed around it during the Iran-Iraq war. The dome had a parabola shape on a three-meter plinth. H/D: 7/8 m. V: 150 m³. Sand dunes were seen in the vicinity of the village. Fig. 5.39.

YC·81 Jaffarabad

The rounded, conical ice house was deteriorating fast, but represented an opportunity to study the construction build-up of walls (too low to be real shading walls) and the dome, outside and inside. The lower part of the dome was particularly spectacular - an almost two meter thick wall built up of mud bricks, which had been damaged by water erosion from the bottom. Fig. 5.40.

H/D: 12/15 m. V: 400 m³. Gradient was 50 degrees. The ice house probably had served the large fort nearby, as well as the village.

YC·82 Shamsabad

A special design feature here was a chimney-like structure at the top of the stepped cone, which sat on a heavy 4.5 meter high plinth. There was a platform of thin tree trunks in and beneath the chimney structure, which enabled the closing of the vent by means of rags or blankets by men standing on the top of the dome. The major danger of collapse for this structure comes from flooding and erosion at the foot of the dome. H/D: 16/23 m - it is one of the largest ice houses in Iran. V: 1500 m³. Gradient: 55 degrees. Fig. 5.41.

YC·83 Berum

The ice dome is a stepped dome, in a design similar to YC·75 Firouzabad and YC·81 Jaffarabad, both also located in the Damghan region. The Berum ice house dome, however, has a 2 meter plinth supporting 20 steps of 0.7 meters each. H/D: 16/19 meters and ice pit volume V about 1200 m³. Fig. 5.42.

The northern top of the dome has fallen down, but the situation is more serious inside, where large quantities of bricks have been removed from the lower part of the inner shell and probably used for houses in the nearby village.

YC·84 Vamerzan

The ice house (H/D: 8/11m, V: 250 m³) is used as a store room for a village house.

YC·85 Qaleh Agha Baba

The original measurements of the conically shaped ice house were estimated at H/D: 8/9 m. The ice house had been converted into a private garage. As no one was home when this site was visited, it was impossible to gain access to the interior of the structure.

Fig. 5.41. YC·82 Shamsabad with tall plinth and chimney

YC·86 Jizan South

This ice house was observed from the bus on the Mashad-Tehran highway, and no firm data were obtained.

YC·87 Imamabad

The existence of this ice house was reported by the taxi-driver who drove me from Shahrud to Damghan, and no firm data were obtained.

YC·88 Behdasht and YC·89 Behdasht II

The two pointed, paraboloid domes were located at a distance of 100 meters from each other. The western example, Behdasht II, was in a more miserable state than the eastern, Behdasht I. They were judged to have been originally of the same size, with an H/D of 12-13/14 m and a gradient of 60+ degrees. The ice pit volume was for each facility estimated to have been about 500 m³. Fig. 5.43.

Fig. 5.42. YC·83 Berum Dome interior

Fig. 5.43. YC·88 Behdasht I
Seen from YC·89 Behdasht II

They were located in an enclosure of 3-4 meter high walls, which were not aligned east-west as is usual for shading walls; the purpose of the enclosure was not clear. In the eastern ice house, wooden struts were found in the inner, rough-surfaced mud brick shell, about three, four and eight meters from the top and just visible at the eroded outer surface. No wood was visible in the western ice house dome, which had almost completely collapsed.

YC·91 Agha Mohamad Lotfi/Dizedj
This example seemed to be more crudely built than others in the area, as it looked lopsided from a northwest angle. H/D: 8/12 m. V: 300 m³. The gradient was 55 degrees. A top vent was visible.

YC·92 Dizedj Central
This ice house had disappeared completely and been replaced by a mosque, in the wall of which a few fragments of the old ice house can still be seen.

YC·93 Garman, YC·94 Mianabad, YC·95 Zargar and YC·96 Chahar Taq
These ice houses were indicated to me by a *Mirâs Farhangi* internal report (of poor quality as copied/photographed by me), which contained their names and photographs. Apart from YC·93 Garman, which I could locate on Google Earth, it is not clear that the others still exist, either complete or in part. It was too late in the survey for a re-visit of the area.

Fig. 5.44. YC·97 Biar Djamand
View from south east

YC·97 Biar Djamand

Despite heavy erosion, the dome design appeared to have been a slightly pointed paraboloid. H/D: 9/15 meters, with a gradient of 55 degrees. V: 500 m³. Fig. 5.44.

Wood inserts were observed at levels of 30, 45, and 60 per cent of the total height of the dome. The ice pit side wall was carefully plastered with *kâh-gel* mortar. The ruin of an attendant's house was situated at the south side of the dome, where a truckload of planting soil had also been dumped. There may thus be the possibility that a park will be established, and the ice house perhaps restored in the near future.

YC·100 Azamabad

The design was a cone, rounded at the top, with an H/D of 7/10 meters, and gradient of 57 degrees. V: 200 m³. Fig. 5.45.

An access path to the top had been carved into the east side of the dome and was a source of erosive action. Wooden struts were

Fig. 5.45. YC·100 Azamabad
View from east

Fig. 5.46. YC·102 Ghasemabad
South side

inserted at levels of 35, 50 and 90 per cent of the total dome height. There were remains of a small auxiliary building at the south-west side of the dome.

YC·101 Dowlatabad Moj

This eroded, paraboloid-shaped ice house, with an access stairway on its south-west side, was located in the middle of a large field. It once supplied large amounts of ice to the town of Bostam, according to my local guide. H/D: 12/17 m. Gradient: 60 degrees. V: 1000 m^3. The upper five meters of the inside of the dome displayed very decorative mud brick work.

YC·104 Ghasemabad

The dome had a paraboloid shape with a chimney-like top, in the style of Dowlatabad (above) and Shamsabad (YC·82). The H/D is 13/18 m, and the gradient changes from 75 degrees at ground level to 55 at the transition to the chimney. V: 1200 m^3. Fig. 5.46.

The dome was eroded down to the mud brick body and had a spiraling stairway on the north side that represented a weak point in terms of erosion by rain and wind.

Fig. 5.47. YC·105 Miami
View from east

YC·105 Miami

The two domes are of similar paraboloid shape, but with H/D of 9/11 and 6/7 meters. Like at Hassanabad (YC·80), near Damghan, the ice houses had been integrated into a martyr cemetery established during or just after the Iraq war in the 1980s. There was a tomb inside the larger western dome. Fig. 5.47.

General comments · Semnan Province

Semnan Province displayed many different types of domed ice houses. In the western part, about 100 kilometers from Tehran, around Garmsar, stepped cones with a 55 degrees angle on a small plinth were common (YC·55 to YC·63). The same builder, or unit or family of builders, may therefore have built them. The stepped cones require more maintenance than straight, rendered surfaces, but are easier to access and work on. The placing of doors in the domes varied, but they were mostly placed at the east and west sides, yet at YC·57 and YC·59 only at the north side. When moving east towards Semnan town, the ice houses were characterized by plastered paraboloid surfaces, with varying directions of the door openings. East of Semnan, in the Damghan area, stepped surfaces had become fashionable again; and they changed again to paraboloids in the Shahrud area. Most, if not all, ice houses had top vents - at YC·104, almost chimney-like with wood struts, but many vents seemed to have been plugged when the ice houses changed to other uses, or were restored. Dome material was everywhere standard *kâh-gel* mud bricks and mortar. At the two domes at Miami (YC·105), some large stones had been placed on the top of the domes for unknown reasons. They may have been placed on plastic sheeting or tarpaulins which have been carried away by rains and storms.

In all ice pits accessed, the wall and bottom surfaces were made of tamped, untreated soil, with rare local repairs with plaster, and only at YC·75 was a bottom drain channel to be seen. A few domes had wood inserts in the inner shell – Firouzabad (YC·75), Biar Djamand (YC·97), Azamabad (YC·100), Bostam (YC·103), Ghasemabad (YC·104), in some cases going through the dome to the outside, which would have facilitated access for repairs..

As already noted, ice houses with ice-making plant were rare in this part of the Project Area. Only Firouzabad (YC·75) and Abdolabad (YC·76) had shading walls.

Fifteen domed village ice houses (plus the latest caravansary example at Dah Namak, near Garmsar) in Semnan Province had up until 2005 been registered in the National Registry. All were dated to the Qadjar Period (YC·64, 68, 70, 71, 72, 74, 91, 97, 98, 99 and 104), or earlier (YC·73, 88, 90, 101 and one not identified at Bostam). The Semnan Branch of *Mirâs Farhangi* had even prepared appraisal reports for additional entries in the NR. The registration effort in Semnan Province thus was adequate, but in no case had the registration effort been followed up by conservation. All Semnan Province ice houses were in a more or less advanced state of decay and deterioration.

Fig. 5.48. YC·108 Sabzevar I
West side seen from the ring road

Razavi Khorasan Province

Domed ice houses with ice plant
DVP type

YC·108 Sabzevar I

Three large paraboloid domes, with as many as eight associated 50-60 meter-long shading walls, constituted this comprehensive ice house complex five kilometers southwest of the Sabzevaran city centre, at the Bypass Road. All ice house components were much damaged, and a telephone line passed between the domes. The domes – with a few decorative mud brick courses in the inside shell – had an H/D ratio of 15/21 meters, and gradients of 62 degrees. Total ice pit volume was of the order of 5000 m³ (3x1600), and all pits had a ledge at ground level and staircases into the pits, which were dug into the natural subsoil and plastered with *kâh-gel* mortar. Fig. 5.48.

Fig. 5.49. YC·109 Sabzevar II
Effect of shading walls
Aerial view from Google

Fig. 5.50 YC·116 Khaf
View from south

YC·109 Sabzevar II

This complex was situated about 600 meters northwest of Sabzevar I – also at the town bypass road - and appears to have been almost identical to it, with triple domes. This ice house complex had, however, eleven shading walls. The satellite image in Fig. 5.49 shows clearly the shading effect of the remaining walls. This plant is much more damaged than Sabzevar I; the image shows that the two southern domes have collapsed completely and fallen into their respective ice pits.

YC·110 Maidan Gusfand

This former ice house – situated close to the Sabzevar Bypass Road like the two Sabzevar ice house complexes - had been converted into a tea house. However, it appeared to have had dimensions similar to the domes of Sabzevar I and II, i.e. an H/D of 15/21 m, a gradient of 61 degrees, and a former ice pit volume of the order of 1600 m³.

YC·115 Kashmar

The paraboloid dome had an H/D of 12/18 meters and gradient of 58 degrees. The dome contained wood inserts at about levels of 33 and 67 percent of the height. V: 1200 m³. Shading walls extended for 65 meters on the west side and only 10 meters to the east.

YC·116 Khaf

The paraboloid dome had an H/D of 9/12, including a two-meter plinth. It was in the process of restoration on the outer surface (using scaffolding), with alternating layers of mud bricks and plastering. The dome inside, with a top vent, was intact but reinforced by plastering up to a height of two meters above ground level. The ice pit volume was once of the order of 400 m³. Fig. 5.50.

YC·117 Sangan

The Sangan ice house was located on Google Earth and is estimated to have dimensions similar the Khaf ice house, located only 30 kilometers away.

Domed ice house with no ice plant
DVO type

Fig. 5.51. YC·112 Ardoghesh
West door

YC·112 Ardoghesh

The 10/15-meter stepped cone-shaped ice house was located in a private garden and was decaying rapidly. The cone top had disappeared. The dome side gradient was 50 degrees; the ice pit volume was 400 m³. The inner shell of the dome contained two levels of 5 meter-long tree trunks, at levels of 50 and 70 percent of the height of the dome. The dome foundation consisted of two layers of *kah-gel* on the original subsoil. Fig. 5.51.

YC·113 Behrud

The Behrud ice house dome had a smooth, plastered surface except on the lower 2-3 meters where the *kah-gel* plaster had fallen off (probably due to moisture coming up from the ground). The H/D was 12/13 meters; the gradient of the cone surface was 62 degrees. The capacity of the ice pit was once about 500 m³, but was filled up at the time of the survey and used as a combined goat stable and store room. Fig. 5.52.

Fig. 5.52. YC·113 Behrud
View from east

YC·114 Soltanabad

This paraboloid dome had an H/D of 11/11 meters and a gradient of 69 degrees. V: 150 m³. The dome was in a terrible state of decay, but decorative mud brick levels were still visible on the inner surface. Local contacts explained that one more ice house once existed some 200 meters further west, at the former fort. Fig. 5.65.

YC·120 Najmabad

This conical ice house was built of baked bricks and consequently not plastered. It resembled a water reservoir (*âb-anbâr*), but did not have the porch and staircase leading down to a tap at the bottom, typical for a reservoir. The doors were walled up by masonry so that an internal inspection was not possible. There may be a faint chance that there was a descent to the bottom of the reservoir from the nearby building, and the installation might then have been a water reservoir. H/D is 12/16 m, the gradient of the three 30/40/30 percent sections of the height was 65 degrees and of the two meter-plinth, 58 degrees. It may be that this dome never had a vent, or possibly a vent had been plugged after the plant ceased operation. Fig. 5.53.

YC·121 Rahen

This was a somewhat mysterious ice house as it appeared to have been recently converted into a water reservoir with a (locked) porch at the street 10 meters from the dome. The relatively small former ice house paraboloid (H/D is 6/10 meters) had been completely covered with white plaster. Like Najmabad, this installation will have been built of fired bricks. Fig. 5.54.

YC·122 Kowsar

At this location, listed in the National Registry as an ice house, only a restored water reservoir was found. It is unclear whether the ice house had been demolished, or whether the water reservoir had been registered as an ice house.

General comments · Razavi Khorasan Province

The Sabzevar I and II ice house complexes (YC·108 and 109) were quite special in that they each had (had) three large cones and eight or more shading walls. They were huge plants that supplied

Fig. 5.54. YC·121 Rahen
View from the street

probably not only the villages around them, but also travelers on the Silk Road passing the sites, and the town of Sabzevar. The plants were in rapid decay, and at Sabzevar II two of the three large domes – and the top of the third - have collapsed and disintegrated, together with the unlined ice pits, almost without a trace. All of the remaining ice house domes are of a similar size and shape and could well have been constructed by the same builders.

In terms of dome design, the Razavi Khorasan ice houses generally displayed a pointed cone or a paraboloid shape. At Khaf (YC·116), the ongoing rebuilding of the cone, involving the use of baked bricks, probably to be subsequently covered by *kâh-gel* plaster, concealed the original shape and materials used.

All Razavi Khorasan mud brick ice houses appeared to have had ventilation holes at the top of the dome. At Ardoghesh (YC·112, horizontal tree trunks at two levels), Kashmar (YC·115, rings of tree stumps at 3 m height intervals), and Khaf (YC·116, tree branches spread over the inner dome surface), wood had been built into the dome. Most ice houses had doors at their east and west sides, yet at Soltanabad (YC·114) and Kashmar (YC·115) they were located at the north/south and north/east sides, respectively.

At Sabzevar, an imaginative use of the old ice pits occurred. The so-called Maidan Gusfand (YC·110, "Sheep Square") ice house, situated less than a kilometer east of the Sabzevar complexes, had been converted into a restaurant, probably serving traders at the regular sheep markets in the adjacent square. A number of ice houses in Sabzevar – allegedly five, however not identified - had been used as ammunition dumps by the military for almost forty years (Ghobadian 1998: 336).

Three examples of ice houses built of baked bricks occured in the southern part of the province: the village ice house at Najmabad (YC·120), and two caravansary/fort ice houses at Amrani (YC·118 and 119, see below). The reasons for this local use of baked bricks are not clear, but it could be that the area north of Gonabad is plagued by violent storms, sometimes in connection with rain, which would attack and damage mud brick structures. Or, it could be that these ice houses were constructed by water reservoir builders, who traditionally used baked bricks. No vents appeared to have been used in the baked brick ice houses.

The Rahen ice house (YC·121) had been converted into a water reservoir, which confirms the suspicion that it was built of baked

Fig. 5.55. YC·124 Behlgerd

bricks. The thick plaster layer and difficult access made a closer examination impossible. Only at Rahen and Khaf had repair and restoration works been initiated; all other ice houses were left to crumble. For obvious reasons, the baked brick ice houses displayed much greater strength and resistance to decay than the mud brick structures.

South Khorasan Province

Domed ice houses with ice plant
DVP type

YC·123 Shokatabad

This former paraboloid-shaped ice house, with a 50 meter-long curved western shading wall, was in a pitiful state of deterioration. Only the ice pit, with its one meter-ledge at ground level and its six meter deep stone wall, was relatively intact. H/D: 9/12 m. Gradient of the dome surface: 58 degrees. Ice pit volume: app. 500 m³.

Fig. 5.56. YC·127 Birjand SE twin ice
houses
Power line through site

YC·124 Behlgerd

This ice house was very similar to the Shokatabad plant in size, design and state of decay. However, the shading wall is more curved at this site and the ice pit is lined with plaster. Fig. 5.55.

YC·126 Amirabad-Sheivani

This plant was similar to Behlgerd in size, design and state of decay. The ice pit was filled up with collapsed dome material.

YC·127 Birjand SE Twins

This site had twin ice houses, each of a size, design and state of decay similar to the Birjand area plants. And a telephone line passes right through the monument. The ice pits had stone walls. Fig. 5.56 and 5.57.

YC·128 Bojd

One more ice house of similar size, design and state of decay. The ice pit was dug out of the natural sub-soil. No trace of a shading wall existed.

Fig. 5.57. YC·127 Birjand Twins
Ice pit

Domed ice house with no ice plant
DVO type

YC·129 Moalem/Khayam

This was a small ice house, built of baked bricks. It had probably belonged to a private estate at the time of operation and been situated outside town. H/D: 6/19 m, gradient 50 degrees. V: 250 m³.

General comments · South Khorasan Province

The South Khorasan collection of ice houses consisted of five almost identical cone ice houses with curved shading walls around the town of Birjand. All are beautiful examples of the genre, and all are in a rapid state of decay.

In Birjand, furthermore, there was a huge wall at Rahimabad Avenue (YC·125, see below), probably belonging to an underground ice house cellar, which could not be traced. The small domed Moalem/Khayam Street ice house (YC·129), made of baked bricks, is now in the process of being engulfed by expansion of the university campus.

The five mud brick ice houses outside town had ice pits lined with either stone walls and/or plaster.

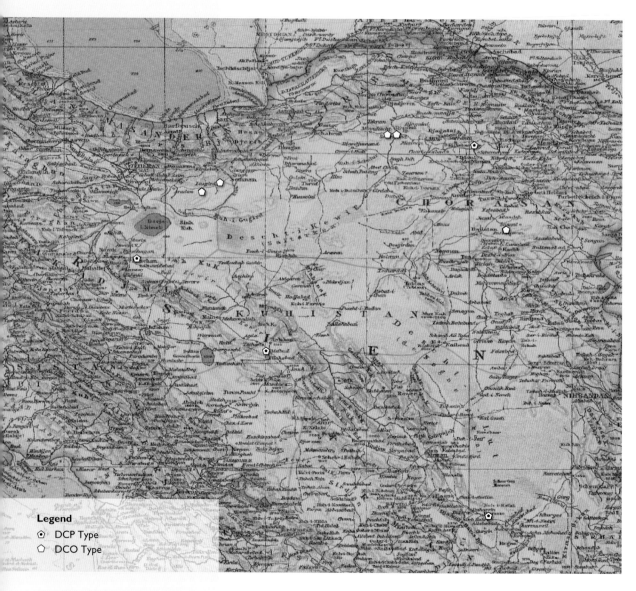

Fig. 5.58. Locations of domed caravan-
sary/fort ice houses. DCP and DCO
types.

Legend
- ⊙ DCP Type
- ○ DCO Type

Domed ice houses at caravansaries or forts DCP and DCO types

While the inventory of domed village houses in many parts of the Project Area can be considered exhaustive, this cannot be said to be true for the other types of ice houses (caravansary and town ice houses) - they are rather to be considered a spinoff of the village ice house search. Water tanks were indispensable for caravansaries; however, it appears only a few caravansaries had ice houses

(*Ganjnameh* Vol. 17, 2005).[30] Of the total of 12 caravansary/fort ice houses identified during the survey, five had ice-making plants (DCP type) and seven had none (DCO type).

Although caravansary ice houses were not a specific target of the survey, and so these numbers are consequently not exhaustive, it appears that the distribution of caravan/fort ice houses largely corresponds to that of domed village ice houses with or without ice-making plant, see map in Fig. 5.58. As in the domed village ice houses, it is notable that the numerical distribution ratio DCP/DCO is of the order of 50/50 percent, and that all DCO (i.e. without ice-making plant) except one (YC·111) are located along the Elburz Mountains in the north, and that all DCP (i.e. with ice-making plant) are located the Kashan-Yazd-Kerman-Bam regions, in the western part of the Project Area. The reason for this particular distribution is believed to be the same as for the village ice houses: It is simpler and cheaper to fetch ice from the mountains, if they are nearby, than to build and operate an ice-making facility with associated water supply systems. Despite their limited number, the distribution of the twelve caravansary/fort ice houses, all domed, thus supports the general picture regarding distribution obtained for the domed village ice houses and described earlier in this chapter.

Kerman Province

YC·31 Bam

The ice house was located northeast of the Citadel of Bam, largely destroyed by an earthquake in December 2003. At that occasion the upper half of the recently restored ice house dome fell down.[31] The remainder of the dome displayed several ornamental mud brick courses.[32] The heavy paraboloid dome had an H/D of 15/22 and gradient of 58 degrees. From the ledge at ground level the restored ice pit was eight meters deep (V: 1800 m³); it was plastered with kâh-gel and had a drain ditch at the bottom. The remains of a maximum 80 meter long shading wall were visible at the west side. In view of the large ice pit volume, the relatively short shading wall for ice-making ponds, and the low annual number of frost days (9 only), it is assumed that the major part of the ice for storage in winter was transported from the nearby mountains. Fig. 5.59.

Fig. 5.59. YC·31 Bam with the destroyed citadel in the background

Yazd Province

YC·34 Meybod

H/D: 18/23 m. Dome shape: a pointed paraboloid. Gradient: 70 degrees. V: 1200 m³. Fig. 5.60.

The dome of the ice house and the ornamented shading wall, as well as the ice pit, have been completely restored. There was an 80 centimeters-wide vent at the top of the dome. On the south side of the dome there were two external staircases to enable access for maintenance of the *kâh-gel* plastered surface, usually undertaken every year but also after heavy rains. The description and photographs of the restoration (with primitive scaffolds) can be found in the Yazd Water Museum. Before the restoration, the ice house dome surface had fourteen external steps, but the outer surface had then been made smooth during restoration. The ice house was part of complete road station, with caravansary, post relay station, water reservoir and restaurant. The complex, together with the nearby citadel, is today a major tourist attraction in the Yazd area.

Fig. 5.60. YC·34 Meybod.
View from south

Isfahan Province

YC·42 Moayedi I and YC·43 Moayedi II
These two paraboloid-shaped ice houses were situated on either side of the old citadel wall of Kashan. They were similar in size, design and materials. H/D: 14/21-22 m, gradient 60 degrees. Ice pit volume of each was 1000-1100 m³. Fig. 5.62.

Both plants were decaying rapidly, the earthen ice pits gradually being filled up with rubbish. With only two ice houses observed in Kashan – there had once been at least seven more, local contacts reported - it was surprising that not one of them is registered in the NR. For each of the two Moayedi ice houses 50 to 80 meters of shading walls remained.

Fig. 5.61 YC·64 Dah Namak
View from east, at caravansary

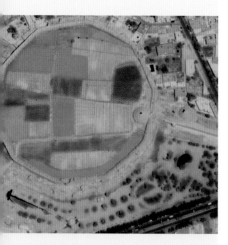

Fig. 5.62 YC·42 and 43. Kashan citadel
wall with two ice houses
Aerial view from Google Earth

Semnan Province

YC·64 Dah Namak and YC·65 Dah Namak Old
The two ice houses each belonged to a caravansary. The most recent caravansary was of Qadjar origin, 100 to 200 years old (*Ganjnameh* 2005: 36). The older caravansary and ice house were probably abandoned when the newer one was built. The two ice houses may well have been of similar size and form; for the more recent the H/D was 10/15 m, the gradient 55 degrees. Ice pit volume was of the order of 500 m³. Fig. 5.61 shows YC·64.

YC·66 Lasjerd
This ice house at the former Lasjerd caravansary was mentioned by the *Mirâs Farhangi* staff, Semnan branch office, but was only seen at a distance from a bus. Coordinates were taken from Google Earth. No other data existed.

YC·106 Abbasabad
This battered roadside ice house consisted of three cone segments, almost miter-shaped, with gradients of 82, 63 and 48 degrees. H/D: 9/11 m. V: 400 m³. There are a large number of wood struts built into the inner dome shell surface at irregular intervals, and horizontal tree trunks cross near the top. Fig. 5.64.
The photograph in Fig. 5.63 was taken from Rainer's *Anonymes*

Fig. 5.63. YC·106 Abbasabad
(c. 1970, Rainer 1977:101)

Bauen im Iran (1977); the text reads: "*Loam buildings and a water cistern which is covered by a mountable dome of loam, at the caravanserai of Abbasabad near Shahrud.*" It is actually an ice house – not a water cistern – and it belonged to the caravansary in the photo. which further shows a number of smaller domed houses of vernacular type. Today the dome is standing isolated at the roadside, and melting.

Fig. 5.64. YC·106 Abbasabad
View from west

Razavi Khorasan Province

YC·107 Sadrabad

Sadrabad was another road side ice house, which was almost completely melted down. It may have been an 8/15 paraboloid and had an ice pit volume of about 200 m^3. Fig. 5.66.

YC·111 Zafaranieh

In a qanat-watered, fertile village with an old caravansary, a 16/22 meters ice house with 40 meters of shading wall, remained, situated 100 meters northeast of an old caravansary. The dome had a four meter plinth base, supporting six steps of two meters, with an average gradient of 55 degrees. The ice pit had a volume of 1200 m^3, but was at the time of the survey inhabited by wild dogs and so not accessible. Beazley thought that the ice house was still in use at her visit in 1970 (Beazley, E., and M. Harverson 1982: 49).

YC·118 Amrani

A small baked brick ice house was found at a small caravansary on the north-south route between Meshad and Birjand. H/D: 5/7m. The gradient of the paraboloid surface: 40 degrees. The decay process is slow because of the resistant baked bricks. There was no access to the inside. During his stay in East Iran during the First World War, the British General W.E.R. Dickson reported: "*As Amrani (village) had a bad reputation as a haunt of robbers… we took special precautions for our cars and their contents.*" (1924: 165)

YC·119 Amrani Fortress

Some 500 meters east of the Amrani ice house was situated a larger one, also made of baked bricks, near the deserted fortified village of Amrani. H/D: 11/18 m. The average gradient of the paraboloid dome was 45 degrees. The pit could not be entered due to the danger of collapse, but seemed to have been lined with baked bricks (Fig. 5.67). The domed ice house found on Moallem Street in Birjand (YC·129) and the two Amrani ice houses are the only examples, out of a total of 104 identified, which were built of baked bricks. Baked bricks are usually used for water reservoirs (*âb-anbâr*) because they can best resist water damage, but normally are not used for ice house structures.

Opposite page
Fig. 5.65. YC·114 Soltanabad

Fig. 5.66. YC·107 Sadrabad
View from south

Fig. 5.67. YC·119 Amrani Fortress
Aerial view from Google Earth

6 | Walled and underground ice houses - description and analysis

Opposite page
YC·16 Jafarabad Jangal

Walled ice houses - WVP and WTP types

If an ice house site had no domed ice pit or ice storage cellar, it was difficult during the field work to decide whether a tall long wall on the site had been the shading wall for ice-making or the shading wall for an ice pit.[33] The indications on the sites were in most cases not sufficient to allow a safe evaluation because the same technique, 0.5 to 0.8 meter layers of mud-straw material (*kah-gel or piseh*) from bottom to top, was used for both types of walls, and the walls were of similar size. However, classification was made on site on a "most probable" basis. Walled ice houses were all judged to have had ice-making facilities, i.e. open-air ponds, but with no walls having shaded the ponds, as none were observed at the five sites found. According to local contacts and the "official" explanation on the Isfahan Town home page, ice was produced in shallow ponds in open fields, without shelter or shade. These extensive space requirements explain why walled ice houses were situated long distances from the city centers.

In the Isfahan area, two walled ice houses were identified outside the city center, near Ateshgah Street. One had disappeared completely and been replaced by residential buildings, as explained by my informant (55 years old), who played on the site as a child. The walls of the other ice house were still standing, but were deteriorating and were exposed to new buildings encroaching on the plant (YC·49 and 48, respectively). Texts indicate that Isfahan once had had an ice house for every quarter of the town, in total about forty walled ice houses in and around town (www.isfahan.ir).[34] In fact, the method of producing and storing ice by means of open ponds and tall walls protecting the ice pit is called the "Isfahan Method".

Only one walled ice house was found in the Tehran area, in a northwest suburb by the name of Kan, about twelve kilometers

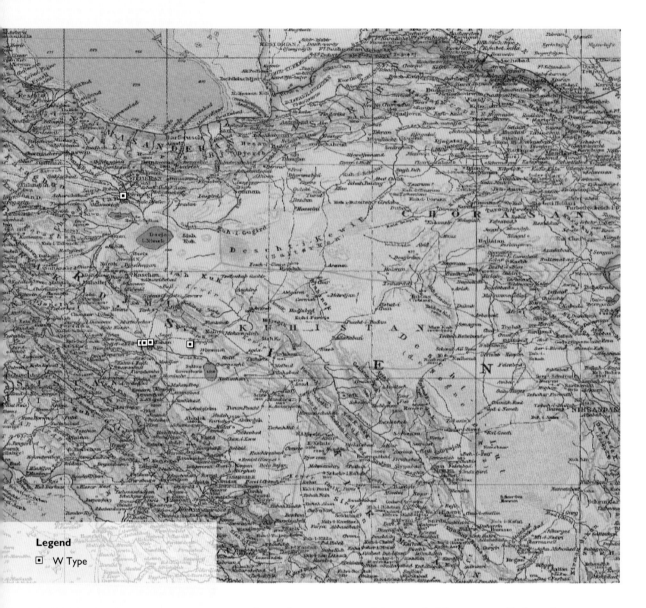

Legend

◉ W Type

Fig. 6.1. Locations of surveyed walled ice houses, one situated near Tehran, and five near Isfahan

from the city center. Most probably more walled ice houses were once situated in the Tehran area, but they are all gone, perhaps because walled ice houses – presumably due to their simple configuration and limited value as industrial architecture – command(ed) no respect in terms of conservation by the authorities and the local people.

Ghobadian asserted that there were no walled ice houses left at the time of his survey (1998: 332); however, this is not the case, as my survey has shown.

Most of the walled ice houses were for general public use, like the water reservoirs (*âb-anbâr*), but unlike the domed village ice

Fig. 6.2. YC·7 Kan near Tehran.
View from east

houses. All walled ice houses probably had ice-making plants, usually in the form of open ponds in the fields around them, unprotected by shading walls (Beazley, E., and M. Harverson 1982: 54). Apart from the one situated at Kan, on the northwestern outskirts of Tehran, all walled ice houses surveyed were situated in Isfahan Province.

Tehran Province

YC·7 Kan.

The ice pit of a length of 80 meters, and a presumed width of 6 meters and depth of 8 meters, was protected by a WNW-ESE aligned wall with 7 meter wing walls at its ends. These dimensions lead to an approximate ice storage volume of 2500 m^3, i.e. of a size which indicates commercial use, probably for Tehran City only ten kilometers away. The plant is in an advanced state of decay and will soon have melted down completely, see Fig. 6.2. The mud used for

Fig. 6.3. YC·48 Ateshgah I at Isfahan
View from east

the wall displayed a significant content of stones and gravel, which makes the wall more vulnerable to erosion if its rendering of purer clay material with straw is not regularly maintained and repaired.

Isfahan Province

YC·48 Kh. Ateshgah I.

A couple kilometers west of the Isfahan city centre, in an region that until 40 years ago was an area of open fertile fields, an 80 meters long and 8 meters tall wall was observed, with a combined entrance and attendant's building at the northeast corner (Fig. 6.3). The almost one meter high kah-gel lifts were still visible in the wall; the decorative parapet at the top was almost gone. The long and tall wall, with its 10 meter long wing walls once protected an ice storage pit of 1500 m^3, which in summer supplied ice to the population of the city. Residential buildings are approaching the site, and it is only a matter of a short time before this ice house will be demolished or transformed into somebody's garden wall.

Fig. 6.4. YC·51 Kuhpayeh I, view from west, near complete destruction

The ice house wall at this site displayed a number of rectangular holes at regular intervals. As they were located on both sides of the wall they could have accommodated a scaffold structure during construction and repairs. Those on the north (ice pit) side could also have served as abutments for temporary roofing to protect the ice pit from the sun when full and backfilled.

YC·49 Khiaban Ateshgah II.
Only a few hundred meters from YC·48 stood a similarly large walled ice house, my driver and friend Ali Nasr explained. Ali lived in the neighborhood as a child. The ice house had been cleared away completely, and only one empty building plot remained in February 2007.

YC·50 Gorat.
The staff at the Isfahan Tourist Office in June 2009 confirmed to me the existence of an "ice house with walls" in the Gorat suburb of Isfahan. No technical data were obtained.

YC·51 Kuhpayeh I.
This ice house was of a design similar to YC·48 above, but in a very

advanced state of disintergration, as the photograph shows. The plant included a 30 meter long main wall and 20 meter long wing walls at each end. According to the local senior citizens (in the photo), ice for storage had been produced in open ponds around the plant. Fig. 6.4.

YC·52 Kuhpayeh II.

This ice house was of a design and size similar to Kuhpayeh I, but in better condition. Parts of the walls were still at full height, about 8 meters. No efforts seem to have been undertaken or planned to preserve this plant.

Like Ateshgah I in Isfahan, both Kuhpayeh ice houses display a series of rectangular holes, which could have served as support for scaffolds during construction and maintenance, or for roofing during the ice storage periods.

General comments, walled ice houses.

It is a disaster that, from a number of more than a hundred walled ice houses in Iran, there were at the time of the survey only four left, and they were declining fast. Only at Ateshgah I (YC·48, Fig 6.3) in Isfahan did an air of dignity still prevail, but the ice house will disappear due to "urban crawl" at the site. Nearby residential buildings are clearly visible in the photo.

As noted earlier, the method of making ice and storing it in pits protected by a wall was called the "Isfahan Method". And, with the exception of the YC·7 Kan ice house, northwest of Tehran, walled ice houses seemed to be an Isfahan area phenomenon.

The home page of the town of Isfahan gives a full description of ice making and storage according to the "Isfahan Method" (www. isfahan.ir), see also chapter 7 in this book.

The W type ice houses are of a very simple design, i.e. a long east-west rectangular storage pit, protected on the south, east and west sides by tall walls providing shade and shelter. At none of the four preserved sites was there any trace of the ice-freezing ponds and water channels, which would have been situated in large areas near the storage.

None of Iran's walled ice houses were admitted into the National Registry, and no walled ice house had been maintained or restored. It is truly and sadly a disappearing piece of industrial architecture.

Underground ice houses
- UVP and UTP types

The absence of traces of underground ice pits and of ice ponds – as was the case at YC·1 Arbab Taghi in Tehran and YC·125 Rahimabad in Birjand - made it difficult to ascertain whether high and long walls had been shading walls for ice making ponds, or whether they had been protection walls for open air ice pits (clamps). In both of the above cases it was assessed that nearby road works and/or building projects had necessitated the demolition of the ice storage cellars, and consequently that the two ice houses had been of the underground type, UTP.

The Tehran area once allegedly had more than eighty ice houses (Ghobadian 1998: 329). They were probably spread around town, as was the case with walled ice houses in Isfahan. Motamedi (2002: 715) lists 20 ice houses – located in central Tehran some 80 years ago – but they have all disappeared. Today only the poor remains of a single example (Arbab Taghi) still exist. Local contacts mentioned an ice house by the name of Imamzadeh Davoud. It could not be located.

All underground houses had associated ice production, but only parts of the shading walls remain, if anything at all.

YC·1 Arbab Taghi, Tehran.
What remains of the ice house complex are two parallel 200 meter-long walls, the remains of which have been integrated into a "modern" park, see Fig. 8. It is believed that the walls once served as shading walls for large ice ponds, with a water supply from qanats, and that there once existed one or more associated underground ice pits/cellars in the neighborhood.

YC·2 Khaniabad.
This could well have been the ice cellar described by Boisen (1946:124), which in the late 1930s was demolished to give space for the new Tehran Railway Station shunting yard.

YC·3 Khalili.
This ice house was included in the National Registry in 1977. An extensive search proved fruitless, and enquiries in the area indicated that it had been demolished "many" years ago when the city expanded.

YC·4 Kh. Ahang and YC·5 Maidan Khorasan.

Several contacts, including the Iranian ambassador to Copenhagen in 2008, explained that fifty years ago there had been more than forty ice houses in this part of Tehran, which Motamedi (2002: 715) confirms generally. An extensive search and many enquiries led to the conclusion that they had all been demolished in connection with the expansion of the city.

YC·6 Gholhak.

When I was living in Gholhak, in northern Tehran, in the 1970s, I passed through the *Khiyâbân-e-Yakhchâl* (Ice House Street) every day, but the ice house was long gone. A fellow guest at a private party in 2008 explained that as a child (about 60 years ago) he and his mother went to the Gholhak ice house to buy ice from a deep cellar near some tall walls.

YC·8 Maidan Fath.

My old friend J.S. Teglbjaerg, who worked in the Old Karaj Road in the 1960s and early 1970s, on his way to and from work passed some huge walls which belonged to an ice house. At that location, at the beginning of the Old Karaj Road, is situated today a huge motorway roundabout, in the middle of which the traces of several parallel and perpendicular lines can still faintly be seen on the satellite imagery. It is believed that this ice house complex had one or more large ice storage cellars. No photographs or field measurements were taken due to the proximity of the Mehrabad Airport.

YC·15 Jaffarabad Jangal.

While all of Tehran's underground ice houses seemed to be tales of the past, the large Jafarabad ice house near the Imam Khomeini Mausoleum, south of Tehran, could still be detected and studied – although it was deteriorating and in great danger. It consisted of a large underground ice cellar, with dimensions of 6 x 8 x 21 meters, i.e. a storage volume of some 1000 m³, covered by a ribbed vault with pointed arches, all in mud brick (Fig. 6.5). The ice cellar was accessible and local people had taken and reused many of the mud bricks of the cellar walls. The cellar was open to the sky as the vaults and one of the supporting arches have collapsed and the material cleared away. The large shading wall, 103 meters long with 10 meter wing walls at each end, was still largely intact, but agriculture activities have encroached

Fig. 6.5. YC·15 Jaffarabad Jangal

to within a couple of meters of the wall and the cellar and are contributing to the ongoing demolition of this spectacular plant.

YC·18 Taghrud.

This ice house, situated about midway between Saveh and Qom, had a cellar with cross vaults on columns in a 6x6 meter grid, all in baked brick. The cellar volume is of the order of 400 m³, which seems small in relation to the three different shading wall systems south and west of the cellar. The strange ratio of only 400 m³ of storage compared with almost 200 meters of shading walls of various heights raises the suspicion that this ice house once had had a larger ice reservoir covered by a dome; however, no evidence for this was observed. The Taghrud cellar roof was covered by just a thin layer of earth (Fig. 6.6).

YC·19 Saveh.

An underground ice house at Saveh was described by Ghobadian (1998:327); however, it did not exist any longer at my visit in 2008. Local contacts explained that the ice house had been situated at the Sugar Factory Road (*Khiyâbân-e-Kârkhâneh-ye-Qand*) in Saveh. They said the ice house had been demolished in recent years to give

Fig. 6.6. YC·18 Tagh Rud
Ice cellar and shading walls

way to a new boulevard and square. The *Mirâs Farhangi* staff at the local museum had no knowledge of an ice house in Saveh, but gave me directions to the domed ice house of Mehdiabad, YC·20.

YC·125 Rahimabad.

A huge wall, whose function was not entirely clear, was found in the town of Birjand. Perhaps there could have been a large ice cellar on the now leveled open field on the south side, i.e. a layout similar to that of Jaffarabad above (YC·15, UTP type). In this case, the large wall would have been a shading wall for ice ponds on the north side, where a large boulevard has now been built. Or, perhaps the tall wall protected an open, deep ice storage pit, which has now been filled up and replaced by the boulevard arrangement, in which case it would have been a WTP type ice house. While satellite images reveal no traces and no hint as to the type of ice house, it was decided to give it the UTP designation.

The map in Fig. 6.7 shows that underground ice houses were primarily a Tehran phenomenon, with only two sites identified in the Saveh-Qom region southwest of the metropolis, and (a presumed) one in Birjand in East Iran.

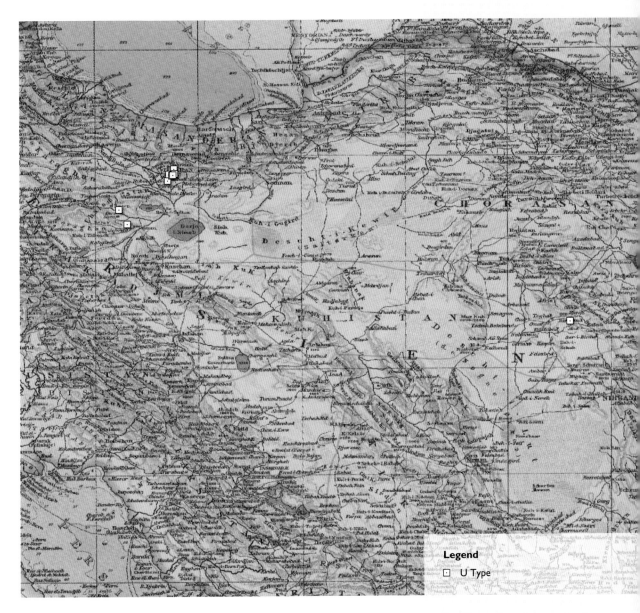

Legend

☐ U Type

Fig. 6.7. Locations of surveyed underground ice houses.

General comments, underground ice houses

... *"The remains of the old ice houses in this area is a symbol of people's effort for the realization of their ideas in spite of difficulties in the work process. And by using their talents and turning difficult tasks into simple works they have left an instructive lesson for coming generations"* ... (Part of text on a memorial plaque in front of the Arbab Taghi ice house (YC·1) in southern Tehran, restored in 1991). Fig. 6.9. This statement sounds promising but the reality is not so positive.

Fig. 6.8 . YC·I Arbab Taghi.
Wall "restored"

Opposite page
Fig. 6.9. Memorial plaque at Arbab
Taghi ice house

- The Arba Taghi ice house has been only partly re-built and at the same time combined with modern arches, beams, columns and pavilions so that it is impossible to recognize the original ice house type and configuration, so, in fact, the ice house has been restored beyond recognition and the determination of its type remains conjectural. As noted earlier, the remains of the two 200 meter-long walls probably once shaded the ice-making ponds of an underground ice house serving the local population on a commercial basis

- There are no traces of the ice-making ponds, the water supply system, and the presumably very large, former ice storage cellar.

- Apart from the memorial plaque at the entrance, users of the park do not get a feeling of visiting an important piece of cultural heritage.

It is a sad fact that of the possibly more than eighty underground ice houses that once served the metropolis of Tehran not one still exists, except the example at Arbab Taghi, restored and rebuilt beyond

بنام خدا

بشر از آغاز محمود طرید ... از آن در شگفت بوده است و با تغییرات ... گوناگون آورده ... دخرشخالی در بار ...

دو حشت فرد ورقه و در همه بوده است که به ... را زور مزطبیت ... پهردنا ... مریشخالی ... مند ... بهراسش پهکامد

انسان با مطالعه دیرشته های تاریخی ... شیوه های تفکر و رفتار پاسه ... دور ... آورده و کاردوست خود را ... یادگاری برای آیندگان باقی ... آنچه در باره ...

فضای خاص ... ای که ... احدی بصورت دیواری ... در زمینه ... شده ... از ... درون شده است که سعی در حفظ ... در ... سعر ...

... آثار ... مانده ... ای ... در محدوده طرح ... روز با از کو بی نماید که در ساخت بر ... خود بطور غم غر ... ساخت ... یادگاری ... آن ... ز شکل ... در های مورد ...

نسلهای آینده به یادگار گذاشته اند این ... در دل تهران ... سده ... از ... رخ در ...

... است که در کان ... را به یادآور می و ... خجل ... با از ...

این مجموعه با طراحی و نظارت آقای نصر ... یزدی و دو سال کار ... برادران ... شهرداری منطقه ...

... شده تا ضمن آسایش ... گذشته را آینده را اجرا به آورد.

شهرداری ...

۱۶ بهمن ۱۳۷۵

recognition. It is further believed that several more underground ice houses existed in the region south-west of Tehran in the direction of Saveh and Qom. The *Mirâs Farhangi* report (1999) mentions that underground ice houses prevailed in towns such as Tehran, Saveh, both within the Project Area, and Hamedan, Zanjan, and Tabriz, to the west. Indeed, as noted above, of the possibly last four underground ice houses still existing in Iran, only two had the remains of ice cellars, and probably not for long. As was the case for the walled ice houses, underground ice houses have no interest in terms of conservation.

In his book about the construction of the Trans-Iranian Railway in the 1930's, Boisen (1946:124) throws some light on the disappearance of the town ice houses. He asked the engineer on site what there was in the large area in southern Tehran before the railway station, the tracks, the shunting yards, and the workshop were built. The engineer answered, *"Ice factories and qanats, the underground water ducts. The ice factories were re-built somewhere else in town. You have probably seen them; they consist of a very tall wall that protects against the rays of the winter sun. Several times during the winter the ice is broken up and placed in large underground cellars where it can keep over the summer. One of these underground chambers in the railway area was very large, not less than 40 meters long, ten meters wide and ten meters deep. During the entire summer there was a constant temperature of about a couple of degrees centigrade. Before the cellar was moved we often went there during the hottest hours to have a little cooling down."* On the question whether or not the qanats were difficult to re-locate, the answer was: *"We didn't move them at all. We lined them with cement blocks so that they would not collapse."*

In fact, no conclusions can be drawn about a general layout of these underground ice houses because so few were found during the survey and they were each quite different. The designs of the two ice cellars that were found are completely different. One (Jaffarabad Jangal) is large, with the cathedral-like cellar built of mud bricks in association with a long, tall shading wall. The layout resembles that of a classical domed village ice house, but a large cellar has replaced the dome and its ice pit. The other example (Taghrud) has a small ice cellar built of baked bricks in association with a number of shading walls of different lengths and heights, all in mud and mud brick material.

Other ice house types

"…throughout the country there are only the local ice houses, whose most important feature is a mud wall at least ten feet high and running in an east-west direction. On the north side of the wall several square pits are dug, and when freezing weather arrives water is put into the pits. Usually the cold will be sufficient to freeze only an inch or two of water during the night, and each day the accumulated ice is broken up and more water added while the high wall prevents the sun's rays from melting the ice during the daytime. After a week or so when each piece of ice is five or six feet thick, it is removed to a special storage chamber under a roof thickly insulated with brush or reeds. Snow is also commonly used during the summer, collected and stored by dwellers in the highest mountain villages, and when hot weather comes, carried on donkey back to the nearest town." (Wilber 1957: 181).

What Wilber described seems to be an underground ice house where the roof is made of twigs, branches, reed and straw. It appears that other types of ice houses than the ones described in this report may have existed in Iran, and that not only ice but also compressed snow was used as a cooling medium in storage. However, such an ice house, with a wooden roof structure with insulation of brush or reeds[35], was neither discovered during the project survey, nor reported by local informants.

In her book *Living with the Desert,* Elizabeth Beazley describes an "ice-pool" located in the shade of a battery of sixteen pigeon towers near Lenjan, outside Isfahan (Beazley, E., and M. Harverson 1982: 110). My search for this special building complex remained unsuccessful, and local contacts confirmed that it had been demolished a couple of years before my visit in 2009.

نحوه حمل یخ از داخل یخچال به خارج آن .

7 | Domed ice houses – technical aspects

Opposite page
Ice house cross section
(Ghobadian 1998: 323)

Configuration

The construction of ice houses follows more or less the same principle (as for water reservoirs), with a shallower and broader well, dug in funnel shape. In the area around an ice house one often finds a channel measuring roughly 110 yards (a hundred meters) in length, thirty feet (ten meters) wide, and roughly one and a half feet (forty to fifty centimeters) deep. This channel is kept in shade thanks to a wall around forty feet (a dozen or so meters) in height, which acts as a screen and is sometimes built in the form of an arch or a circle. (Porter Y., and A. Thevenart 2003:33)

Figure 7.1 illustrates in broad outline the cross section and plan of an ice house near Yazd, drawn up by the British architect Elizabeth Beazley during her survey around 1970. The ice house is very similar to the Meybod ice house (YC·34), which is classified as a domed ice house belonging to a caravansary or fort (i.e. DCP), because it is situated at the old Meybod road station complex. But the layout and the section are typical as well for the many domed village ice houses (DVP), which the survey has confirmed (see also the general description in Chapter 1).

The ice house in Fig. 7.1 represents the classical and most common configuration of the DVP/DCP type, which displays a dome with an east-west running straight shading wall, touching the dome at the wall's south side. Doors in ice house domes were most often placed in the west and east sides of the dome, and towards the north, but seldom at the south side of the domes as that will always be the sunny and hot side. There are slight variations to this layout: If a shading wall was not oriented east-west, then it was turned slightly clockwise to better protect against the afternoon sun (e.g. YC·7 Kan and YC·12 Hakimabad). In addition, dome and wall can be reversed so that the dome is on the wall's north side, and at some sites the shading wall does not extend beyond both sides of the dome, but is only on one side, either because

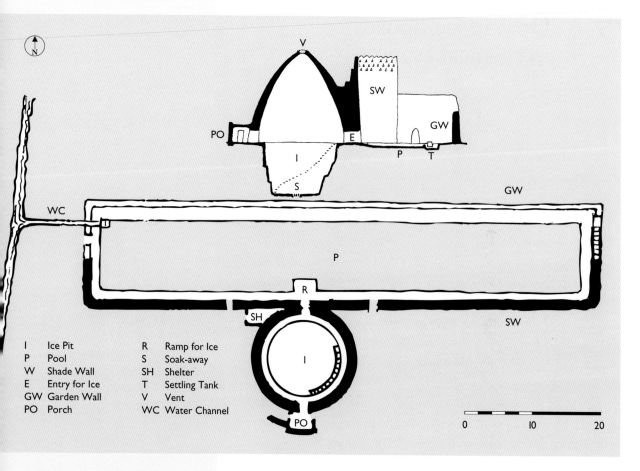

I   Ice Pit   R   Ramp for Ice
P   Pool   S   Soak-away
W   Shade Wall   SH   Shelter
E   Entry for Ice   T   Settling Tank
GW   Garden Wall   V   Vent
PO   Porch   WC   Water Channel

Fig. 7.1. Cross section and plan of a "classical" DVP or DCP ice house (after Beazley et al. 1982: 51)

it was built in that manner or because a large section of the wall was torn down to give way to new roads or buildings (e.g. YC·27 Rigabad in Kerman, see later)[36]. Accordingly, classical DVPs and DCPs include: YC·11, YC·12, YC·17, in the province of Tehran; YC·24, YC·25, YC·26, YC·28, YC·30, in the province of Kerman; YC·34 at Meybod; YC·42 and YC·43, at the Citadel wall of Kashan; YC·43, YC·40, YC·46, in Isfahan Province; YC·75, YC·76, YC·99, YC·102, in Semnan Province; and YC·111, YC·115, and YC·117, in Razavi Khorasan Province.

A variation to the above "classical" model displays curved shading walls, probably to give shade during the early and late hours of the day in a manner similar to the wing-wall additions found at some straight shading walls. Domed ice house sites with curved shading walls (all DVP type) include: YC·21, YC·23, YC·27, YC·32, and YC·33, in the province of Kerman; YC·103 and YC·116, at Shahrud and Khaf, respectively, in Razavi Khorasan Province; and all the domed ice houses near Birjand, in South Khorasan Province - YC·123, YC·124, YC·125, YC·126, YC·127, and YC·128.

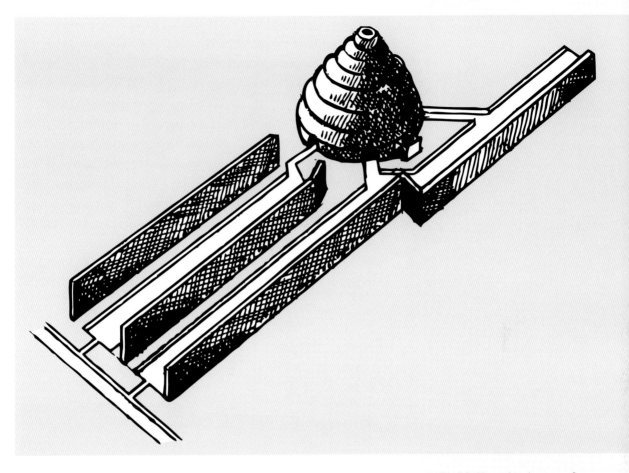

Fig. 7.2. Abarqu I ice house configuration (after Ghobadian 1998: 322)

A group of domed ice houses had several parallel shading walls, as shown already in Fig. 1.2. Fig. 7.2 shows a schematic of the same ice house, YC•37 Abarqu I, with its three parallel shading walls and the water supply system (Ghobadian 1998: 322). The following ice houses (all DVP) were found to have (had) several shading walls: YC•13 Robat Karim, YC•37, YC•38, YC•39, all at Abarqu (each with three shading walls), and YC•108 and YC•109, at Sabzevar (each with originally three domes and with eight and eleven shading walls, respectively). Fig. 5.49, a Google Earth image of the Sabzevar II ice house complex (YC•109), illustrates this type of layout. As noted in Chapter 5, the Sabzevar II ice house plant (YC•109), situated only 500 meters away at the Sabzevar Ring Road, seems to have been identical to Sabzevar I as regards the three domes, but two of the three domes have collapsed and disappeared into the former ice pits. In a few years time, all three domes will have disappeared without a trace.

As regards the domed ice houses without ice-making plant, the simpler layout does not seem to have been an important issue. This type was sometimes located near village centers (e.g. Tarshanbeh, YC·10), in village outskirts (e.g. Sudaghlan, YC·60), and occasionally in the middle of an open field (e.g. Ghasemabad, YC·104).

Ice had to be insulated and kept dry, and so ventilation was very important. The wind blowing across the dome would suck air out at the vent; however, no indication was found of how the domes were protected in case of bad weather (except one near Damghan where there was a wooden grill to support a cover). Presumably, before a rainstorm sacking would be wrapped around the top of the dome to keep the water out. At any rate, constant evaporation through the mud brick dome shell would reduce both humidity and temperature inside the dome.

Dome shapes

Fig. 7.3 shows typical examples of the domes encountered during the survey. The shapes vary greatly in the spectrum between pure cones and paraboloids for the 94 domed ice houses surveyed. As could be seen from the descriptions in Chapter 5, the majority are termed paraboloids, some with tapered and others with smooth surfaces, but not one particular shape could be judged to prevail. There also seems to have been no significant difference between the shape of ice house domes standing alone (DVO and DCO) and the shape of domes having associated shading walls for ice-making ponds (DVP and DCP). The basic principles determining the shape are partly the need to use a form, which will be self-bearing during construction, as there would usually be no wood for support, and partly the need to arrive at an outside shape that minimizes the surface towards the sun and at the same time having a certain height. The higher the dome, the better the cooling effect at the bottom, due to what Hourcade calls "the thermal piston" (1994:93).

In terms of stability and bearing capacity, a dome with a paraboloid cross section is the best and, the higher, the better, also as regards cooling effect. But the building process puts a limit on the height and that limit seems to be about 18 meters, as I could observe during the survey. However, to obtain stability against buckling, i.e. to ensure that no tension forces occur in the dome, the dome must

YC·10 Tarshanbeh

YC·21 Ravar

Fig. 7.3. Dome shapes

YC·26 Moayeri

YC·33 Mahmoudabad

YC·38 Abarqu II

YC·42 Moayedi I

YC·101 Dowlatabad Mo'j

YC·111 Zafaranieh

Fig. 7.4. Plate cover dome, diam. 30 cm

have a certain thickness, and when the dome has a certain thickness and weight, variations of the ideal shape can be used without the danger of tension cracks and ruptures at the surface. The clay building material cannot withstand tension forces, only compression.

None of the ice house domes had a spherical shape, i.e. a circular arch cross section. There appear to be three main reasons for preferring pointed domes: a) the height of the ice house dome is important to create as great a temperature gradient between the (cool) bottom and the (hot) top of the dome (see Hourcade above); b) a spherical shell is not the optimum shape for the combination of necessary strength and minimum weight, i.e. a pointed dome saves weight[37]; and c) the shape of the dome should minimize the surface facing the sun in the middle of the day. For a dome only exposed to its own weight, Mathiasen and Reitzel (1999: 79) show that for an H/D ratio of around 70 percent the material volume of the dome structure is at its minimum, compared with rounder or flatter dome shapes. If this logic is transferred to the three-dimensional world of ice house domes, it may indicate that it is no coincidence that ice house domes are pointed arches, or curved cones, or paraboloids, with the height usually being 65 to 80 percent of the diameter at ground level. However, it is suggested that ice house domes have found their shapes over time by trial-and-error practice, not on the basis of theoretical calculations.

As noted above, one of the reasons for using a pointed dome shape for ice houses is the wish to minimize the surface against the sun. A conical dome shape exposed to the sun, or nearly, will only project its circular base on a plane perpendicular to the sun's rays. The photograph in Fig. 7.4 (from my home) is shown as an example of how close the projection towards the sun of a pointed dome is to the projection of hemispherical dome. With an average dome gradient of 70 degrees, and with a maximum sun height over the horizon of 78 and 82 degrees in Tehran and Kerman respectively, the dome's projected surface against the sun will remain at its minimum for two to three hours around noon-time in summer. The vent at the top of most domes also served as ventilation and could be accessed by means of a stepped dome surface or an external spiral staircase in order to place jute or fabrics for protection against rainstorms.

Most of the tall ice house walls were more than two meters thick at the bottom (e.g. YC·34, 37, 38, and 39), and, at some of the most solid domes with plinths, the thickness at the base could be up to three meters (e.g. YC·12). The use of a plinth as a base for the dome in several cases - YC·26, YC·27, YC·28, YC·30, YC·31, YC·32, all in Kerman Province, and YC·77, YC·79, YC·80, YC·82, YC·83 in the Damghan area - has added to the structural volume and strength, indicating that in these areas savings of materials and work input was not the most important issue.

Dome dimensions

In connection with each ice house site visit, despite the often difficult conditions, it was endeavored to get a reasonable idea about the
main dimensions of the domes, the pits and the walls. The complete
results are contained in the original Ice House Catalogue.

The dimensions – heights and diameters – of the project's ice
house domes have been the subject of a particular analysis. The table in Fig. 7.5 contains the dome dimension data for the 85 domed
houses for which dimensions could be measured or, as in most cases, simply estimated.

On the basis of these dimensions, diagrams were drawn in
which heights and diameters for the domed ice houses of each
province involved in the project are plotted against each other (see
Fig. 7.6). The average curve for the H/D relation has been calculated for Semnan Province, with the largest number of domed
ice houses, and the same curve – the Base Curve - subsequently
copied into the corresponding diagrams for the other provinces,
in order to enable a comparative analysis. The Base Curve shows
that the average gradient varies from 0.71 for the smallest domes
to 0.73 for the tallest. Taking the Base Curve as a benchmark, a
plot above the curve means than the dome in question is more
"pointed" than the Semnan average, and if a plot is below the
curve it means that the dome is "flatter" than the average. The following comments relate to the comparison of the ice house plots
with the Base Curve:

- Tehran Province: The five domed houses located in the province follow generally the Base Curve, however with YC·13 Robat Karim and YC·17 Koleyn being smaller and flatter than the
  larger ones.
- Markazi Province: YC·20 Mehdiabad is of a size similar to Robat
  Karim and of a (restored) shape similar to Koleyn, in Tehran
  Province, the latter two situated 53 to 56 kilometers away towards the northeast.
- Kerman Province: Deviations of domes from the Base Curve
  in Kerman Province are due to the extended use of plinths, on
  which domes of conventional dimensions were placed. The larger domes are of the same approximate size as the much-damaged
  Bam ice house (YC·31, H/D 15/22 mm). Of the non-plinth ice

ID No.	Province	Name	D:Diam. (m)	H:Height (m)	Gradient (degr.)	H/D ratio
10	THR	Tarshanbeh	16	12	55	0.75
11		Aliabad	17	14	70	0.82
12		Hakimabad	22	15	45	0.68
13		Robat Karim	14	9	60	0.64
17		Koleyn	16	11	45	0.69
20	MAR	Mehdiabad	13	9	55	0.69
21	KERMAN	Ravar	16	11	45	0.69
23		Anar	16	12	60	0.75
24		Rafsanjan	16	12	45	0.75
25		Kabutar Khan	13	13	60	1.00
26		Moayeri	21	15	55	0.71
27		Rigabad	21	13	45	0.62
28		Zarisf	22	16	65	0.73
30		Langar/Mahan	16	13	55	0.81
31		Bam Citadel	22	15		0.68
32		Sirjan	13	10	57	0.77
33		Mahmoudabd	16	12	60	0.75
34	YAZD	Meybod	23	18	70	0.78
37		Abarqu I	21	18	55	0.86
38		Abarqu II	20	17	65	0.85
39		Abarqu III	22	18	60	0.82
40	ISFAHAN	Mazreh Drum	16	13		0.81
42		Moayedl I	21	14	60	0.67
43		Moayedi II	22	14	60	0.64
45		Mahabad	22	17	65	0.77
46		Zavareh	12	11	70	0.92
53		Nain	15	12	60	0.80
55	SEMNAN	Ghatul Bozorg	22	13	55	0.59
56		Ghatul Kuchek	9	7	55	0.78
57		Rikan	13	11	55	0.85
59		Shah Sefid	12	9	55	0.75
60		Sudaghklan	8	6	65	0.75
61		Yahteri	12	9	65	0.75
62		Padeh	15	11	65	0.73
63		Imamz.Zoalef	9	7	55	0.78
64		Dah Namak	15	10	55	0.67
65		Dah Namak O	15	7		0.47
70		Zaveghan	15	10	55	0.67
71		Shah Djugh K	7	5	15	0.71
72		Shah Djugh B	16	10		0.63
73		Ateshgah	13	10		0.77
74		Mahaleh Chup	16	12		0.75
75		Firouzabad	20	15	58	0.75
76		Abdolabad	15	12		0.80
77		Alyan	16	13	58	0.81
78		Mohammad-A	12	9		0.75
79		Forat	16	13	45	0.81

Fig. 7.5 A.
Dome dimensions

Fig. 7.5 B
Dome dimensions

ID No.	Province	Name	D:Diam. (m)	H:Height (m)	Gradient (degr.)	H/D ratio
80	SEMNAN	Hassanabad	8	7	60	0.88
81		Jaffarabad	15	12	50	0.80
82		Shamsabad	23	16	45	0.70
83		Berum	19	16	60	0.84
84		Vamerzan	11	8	53	0.73
85		Qaleh Agha B	9	8	45	0.89
88		Behdasht	14	13	60	0.93
89		Behdasht II	14	12		0.86
90		Sa'adabad	9	8	61	0.89
91		Agha M Lotfi	12	8	55	0.67
97		Biar Djamand	15	9	58	0.60
99		Mazdj	18	12	68	0.67
101		Dowlatabad M	17	12	60	0.71
103		Bostam	16	13	55	0.81
104		Ghasemabad	18	13	58	0.72
105		Miami I	11	9	60	0.82
105		Miami II	7	6	60	0.86
106		Abbasabad	11	9		0.82
107		Sadrabad	15	8		0.53
108	R.KHORAS	Sabzevar I	21	15	62	0.71
109		Sabzevar II	21	15	62	0.71
110		Maidan Gusf.	20	15	61	0.75
111		Zafaranieh	22	15	55	0.68
112		Ardoghesh	15	10	50	0.67
113		Behrud	13	12	62	0.92
114		Soltanabad	10	6	69	0.60
115		Kashmar	18	12	53	0.67
116		Khaf	12	9	58	0.75
118		Amrani	7	5	40	0.71
119		Amrani Fort.	18	11	45	0.61
120		Najmabad	16	12	58	0.75
121		Rahen	10	6		0.60
123	S.KHORAS	Shokatabad	12	9	58	0.75
124		Behlgerd	12	9	56	0.75
126		Amirabad-Sh.	12	9	58	0.75
127		Birjand SE Tw	12	9	58	0.75
128		Bojd	12	9	58	0.75
129		Moalem/Kh.	10	6	50	0.60

houses, YC·23 Anar and YC·33 Mahmoudabad appear similar to each other in size (12/16m), as well as in design and in degree of decay.

- Yazd Province: The three Abarqu village ice houses (YC·37, 38, 39) and the Meybod caravansary ice house (YC·34) are the tallest in Iran, i.e. 17 to 18 meters (The height of YC·37 Abarqu I is 18 meters, not 22 meters as indicated on the official plaque outside the ice house). With an H/D ratio of around 85%, the three

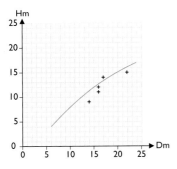

Tehran province

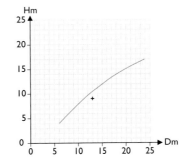

Markazi province

Fig. 7.6 H/D curves

No. of Ice Houses: + ○ ⊕ ✛ ●
                    1 2 3 4 5

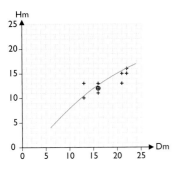

Kerman province

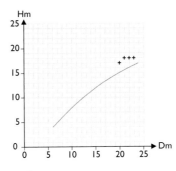

Yazd province

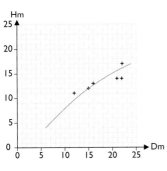

Isfahan province

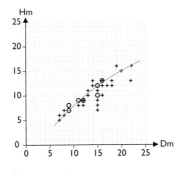

Semnan province

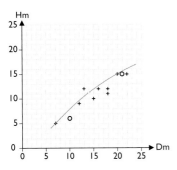

Ravazi Khorasan province

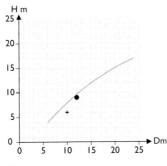

Khorasan province

Fig. 7.7.
Distribution of dome external diameters

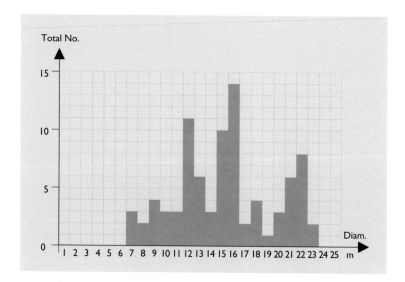

Abarqu ice houses are the most "pointed" of the large Iranian ice
houses.

- Isfahan province: Only the severely damaged ice house at Mahabad (YC·45) seems to have had a size comparable with the Yazd
province ice houses, but it had no ice-making plant (Fig. 5.25).
- Semnan Province: The forty ice houses surveyed show a wide variation in sizes; from "smaller" 5/7 meter models up to 13/18 meter sizes, plus a few 15/20+ meter shapes at Shamsabad (YC·82),
Ghasemabad (YC·104), Firouzabad (YC·75) and Berum (YC·83).
Common sizes appear to have been around 7/9 meters (4 examples), 9/12 meters (6), 10/15 meters (3), 12/15 meters (9).
- Razavi Khorasan Province: At Sabzevar, the two complexes
(YC·108 and 109), each with three large ice houses of 15/21 meter size, are only matched in size by the nearby Maidan Gusfand
ice house (YC·110, now a tea house) and the ice house at the
caravansary of Zafaranieh (YC·111), 30 kilometers farther east.
- Khorasan Province: The area around the town of Birjand includes five ice houses of the same size (9/12 m). This may indicate that a local, fixed model has been used, and perhaps even
the same builder.

In order to obtain an image of the distribution of ice house sizes
within the entire project area, the histogram in Fig. 7.7 summarizes
the data for the prevalence of particular external diameters. The diameter of an ice house is important because it is both a measure of
the size of the dome and of the volume of the ice storage pit.

Fig. 7.8. YC·112
Ardoghesh dome foundation

As can be seen, the most frequent dome diameters are 12-13 meters (17 nos., 20%), 15-16 meters (24 nos., 28%), and 21-22 meters (14 nos., 16%). When assuming a dome wall thickness on average from 1.5 meters to 3.0 meters for the three size categories, and a pit depth of 6 meters, the corresponding ice pit volumes would be:

- For dome diameters 12-13 meters, the ice pit volume is of the order of 400 m³.
- For dome diameters 15-16 meters, the ice pit volume is of the order of 600 m³.
- For dome diameters 21-22 meters, the ice pit volume is of the order of 1100 m³.

Dome foundations and materials

As the field work did not include excavation, no exhaustive account of the foundation methods for domes and walls could be made. However, visual inspection allowed in some cases an assessment of the construction methods of foundations. It did not appear that foundations were ever very deep below the surface (0 to 50 cm), which was always very level at the ice house sites.

Fig. 7.8 shows the interior of YC·112 Ardoghesh, in the Nishabur region, Razavi Khorasan Province. The inner brick wall is placed directly upon two 50 centimeter-layers of *kâh-gel* material (sometimes called pisé/piseh), which in turn sits on a wider, irregular strip foundation of *sefteh* with stone temper (see below for the composition and properties of *kâh-gel* and *sefteh*).

At another location (YC·38 Abarqu II), the *sefteh* foundation layer contained gypsum and lime for reinforcement, and stone temper, and appeared as strong as concrete. This solution was probably widely used, but it could not be verified by visual inspection. Crushed stone fragments were seen in some wall foundations, but more often the wall simply sat on the ground without a foundation.

Clay was used everywhere. This material is easily shaped; it is flexible, practically impermeable, and ideal for climate protection. And it can sustain shrinkage due to variations in water content by means of simple reinforcement with chaff. Clay as building material – when placed in a structure in compression – can resist most of nature's forces. Wind, sand storms, sunshine and frost will do little harm to vernacular mud structures. However, heavy rain showers – as they occur on the Iranian Plateau - can damage the surface, and constant maintenance is required. Of course, the recent violent earthquake at Bam, in December 2003 – the citadel and town were completely destroyed – illustrated once again that earthquakes can easily destroy traditional mud brick structures; however, the greatest danger today comes from the bulldozer.

The construction elements that could be confirmed by visual above-ground on site inspection are listed below (see Wulff 1966: 108ff):

(a) Lime mortar (*sefteh*) for foundations. At a few locations, the lower part of the dome walls, or of the shading walls, had been damaged (and no repair made) and it was therefore possible to study part of the foundations. As was the case for common mud brick buildings in the villages, a simple foundation was made for the dome walls and the shading walls - an approximately 50 centimetres-deep trench was excavated, slightly wider than the planned thickness of the wall, and the excavated earth was carefully gathered at a nearby spot where it was mixed with burnt lime and water to form a soft paste. A layer of about 15 centimetres of this paste was then placed in the trench and a coarse stone temper thrown into it. Once the layer of stones had been placed, a second layer of mud paste with stone temper was added, and this was repeated until the foundation trench was filled (Wulff 1966:108). After a few weeks for the setting of the foundation, the construction of the wall would begin. The *sefteh* was noted to be very firm and compact at several sites (e.g. YC·38, 25, and 57). A foundation trench was not always used, and in several instances the wall was simply constructed on the surface or on a layer of crushed rock, as seen in the photograph of the Ardoghesh ice house (Fig. 7.8).

(b) Straw-mud mix (*kâh-gel*) for walls, mortar, and surfaces. For the building of simple straight or curved walls, so-called pisé or rammed earth walls, clay was moistened and mixed with chaff, tread upon by barefooted labourers, and kneaded into a plastic mass. For walls, this mix was carried to the building site in baskets or thrown in lumps to the builder, who placed it into position. When a course (up to c. 1 meter high) was finished, it was left to set and harden for a couple of days, and the next one was laid, and so on until the desired height had been reached. Wulff explains that the tallest walls made in pisé were the shading walls of the ice houses (1966: 108). These walls were battered slightly as they rose, and became thinner at the top, so that the wall would tend to consolidate itself with age (Michell 1978: 137). For mud brick masonry a *kâh-gel* paste of similar composition was used for mortar, usually placed in 2 cm layers. *Kâh-gel* paste was also used to form the outer shape over the dome shells and for surface plastering of domes and walls. It was particularly important to keep external surfaces intact (i.e. repaired) to avoid deeper erosion damage. The chaff content of the *kah-gel* helped reduce shrinkage and the formation of cracks in dry periods.

(c) Mud bricks (*khest*), sometimes called adobe.[38] Mud bricks are found everywhere in vernacular buildings, even as fill or reinforcement of tall walls (see for instance Fig. 5.21). Mud bricks are made of *kâh-gel*, the same material as used for mortar and pisé walls. The clay is kneaded into a soft paste, which is placed in wooden moulds on the ground and covered with a thin layer of chaff. After the bricks had been left in the sun for a few hours, they were set on edge for further drying and subsequently used for building after a couple of days. The size of mud bricks encountered during the project was 25x25x5 centimetres, with small local variations. This is a good size for building domes and arches, as they offer a large bonding surface and good shaping flexibility, due to their relative thinness.

(d) Lime mortar (*sarooj*). At Ardoghesh (YC·112), Abarqu II (YC·37), and Mahmoudabad (YC·33), there were signs of the use of *sarooj*, a mortar and plastering material, which was predominantly used to render surfaces water impermeable. It was used, for instance, on the surface of the baked brick walls of many water reservoirs. *Sarooj* was - and is still - made as a mud paste (clay, silt, sand), with lime, ashes, egg white, and fine plant fibres or goat hair added for strength and possible impermeability. Hydraulic lime mortar (to "harden under water"), for use especially in the construction of bridges, was introduced to Iran by Roman engineers captured by the Sassanid King Shapur I (242-272 AD) (Frye 1976: 254). Non-hydraulic lime mortar (needs air to carbonate and therefore set) was used even before the Parthian Period (129 BC – 242 AD) (Wulff 1966: 105). During the Parthian and Sassanian Periods, vaulting achieved high technical and architectural standards in public and private buildings (Grube 1978: 134); mortar manufactured from lime, wherever available, was especially preferred for the foundations and corners of the buildings (Wulff 1966: 125).

Forces and volumes

Calculations were carried out on the volumes of mud and mud bricks, and of foundation pressure, at YC·38 Abarqu II, which has a relatively simple shape with reasonably exact dimensions, in order to understand how such simple foundations could support such large structures. The table in Fig. 7.9 contains the relevant data for this ice house and assumptions made for elements that could not be seen and surveyed. Assumptions included the size of the mud bricks used (25x25x5 cm) and mortar joints of an average of 2 cm thickness. Furthermore, it was assumed that two thirds of the dome consisted of mud brick work and the rest of clay mortar and plaster.

These calculations in the table indicate the following results and correlations:

· The foundation pressure at ground level is 11.4 tons/m^2 [39], which is modest as it corresponds to the foundation pressure of a two-storey residential building on strip foundations under "standard soil" conditions.

Height of conical dome:	17 m	Ext. diameter:	20 m	Int. diam.: 16 m
Volume of ice pit:	1000 m³	Shading walls: 3 x 65 m		Height walls: 8 m
Volume of ice-making ponds:	3 x 6 x 0.5 = 585 m³	Clay density:	1.8 t/m³	
Diameter of vent:	0.8 m			
Mud brick dimensions:	25 x 25 x 5 cm	Volume:	0.003125 m³	
Muid brick volume including 2 cm joint:	27 x 27 x 7 cm	Volume:	0.005103 m³	

Assumption: 2/3 of conical dome made of mud brick work

Conical dome volume: vol.cone h/d 19/20 – vol. cone h/d 19/16 = 716 m³
Foundation surface area: area diam. 20 m – area diam. 16 m = 113 m²

Conical dome foundation pressure: 716 x 1.8/113 = 11.4 T/m²

Volume of mud brick work: 2/3 x 716 = 477 m³

Number of mud bricks in conical dome:477/0.005103 = 93,474, rounded off to 94,000

Shading walls volume: 5.75 m3/m x 3 x 65 = 1121 m³
Shading wall foundation pressure: 1121 x 1.8/3/65/2 = 5.2 t/m²

Assumption: Ice-making ponds cross section: width 6 m, depth 0.5 m

Ice-making ponds volume: 3 x 65 x 6 x 0.5 = 585 m³

Fig. 7.9. Pressure and volume calculations for YC·38 Abarqu II

- The foundation pressure at ground level for the eight meter tall shading walls, with a width at the top of 30 cm, is half of that of the dome, i.e. 5.2 tons/m². This is very feasible and explains why it was not necessary for several ice house shading walls – and all the tall garden walls in the villages – to have substantial foundation trenches.
- The volume of the ice house dome structure is 716 m³, which means that the excavation of the ice pit (1000 m³) would have delivered sufficient raw material for bricks, mortar and plaster forming and surfacing. However, material for the dome was probably taken from a nearby borrow pit, as excavation of the deep ice pit was probably not made before the dome was built, for safety reasons.
- The material excavated for the ice pit (1000 m³) was later used for the building of the three 65 meter long shading walls, which required 1121 m³. The soil (585 m³) excavated for the ice-making ponds alone could not cover this amount. Anyway, the earth borrow pits were probably used to a great extent in order not to complicate building site traffic with internal shifting of soil.

Surplus soil would have been returned to the borrow pits at the end of the construction work.

- The number of mud bricks required was 94,000. If, during construction, the rate of brick-making and especially brick-laying were of the order of 1,000 bricks per day – which is probably on the low side – then it would have taken three months to complete the brick work.

- The volume of the ice-making ponds was 585 m³, i.e. one batch of ice was not enough to fill the ice pit of 1,000 m³. Two batches were necessary, or ice had to be procured from the outside to cover an ice deficit. The issue of production times and procurement options will be explored further later in this chapter.

Dome construction

All village ice house domes surveyed were made of mud bricks which were set in mud mortar. For larger domes the mud bricks were built up in two, or even three brick-widths, which were subsequently plastered with mortar on the outside for weather protection. Fig. 7.10 (YC·29 Rikan) offers a splendid view of a dome wall cross section. The image also shows how the partial demolition has led to lack of cohesion and subsequent rupture due to tension forces in the three layer shell.

The ice house domes generally seem to have been built up without the use of scaffolding or supports. By building up first the inner dome shell by successive rings of mud bricks, with each subsequent ring only protruding a few centimeters (in Abarqu III, +/- 1 cm) from the base, and with one or two more mud brick shells stuck to the outside of the inner shell, and by backfilling with mud mortar layers as rendering (plaster) on the outside, a stable structure in compression was maintained during the whole process. As was noted earlier, the weight of the corbelled mud brick shell structure up to the very top was easily absorbed by distribution downwards and sideways through the massive structure into the ground, and including the weight of the builders, which was negligible in comparison. Fig. 7.11 illustrates a similar process in the construction of a corbelled dome in Northern Syria. The builders sit or stand on finished courses in the process of adding further courses of brick and mortar. Presumably the same method was used for the construction of the

Fig 7.10. YC·57 Rikan
Partial demolition and impending
collapse.

Iranian ice house domes. In addition, at the Iranian ice houses the outside of the dome was shaped in a way to allow access without supports, or a set of stairs was cut into the surface for easy access.

After the bricklaying – in one, two and sometimes three brick-widths - the inner dome wall was covered with a mud/straw mix, possibly with mud brick temper, to form the outer shape of the structure. The outer surface was then plastered with a finishing layer of mud-straw mix. The straw (or sometimes chaff) content of the mud mixture acts as a kind of fibre reinforcement, which reduces the shrinkage fissures that occur on the surface after periods of sunny, dry weather. Ordinarily the plastered surface must be renewed every year or immediately after heavy rains (Michell 1978: 137). The discontinuation of such maintenance will inevitably lead to increased deterioration, as I could observe at the majority of the domed ice houses. Wulff reported that the mortar was in places reinforced and made impermeable by mixing burned lime into it (1966:126). No such lime mortar was observed at any ice house, except for the example at Rahen Gonabad (YC·121), where the old ice house had been converted into a water reservoir. In addition to detrimental climatic action, in the form of rain showers, storms and the occasional

Fig. 7.11. Building of a domed house
in Northern Syria (Puett 2005:98)

earthquake, flooding of the ice house interior can lead to erosion of the foundation and subsequent deterioration (see Fig. 7.12).

The thickness of the ice house dome varied from 1.5 meters to 3 meters at the base, and even more when plinths were used as the solid base of domes. The wall thickness gradually diminished to about 30 centimeters – the width of a mud brick and plaster - at the top. At the top, the ice house wall would be a straight continuation of the dome side, or a curve upwards, to ensure a stable structure despite a vent hole in the middle.

In general the building materials used for caravansary ice houses were identical to the ones used for village ice houses. The only exceptions were the ice houses at the Amrani Caravansary and Amrani Fortress in South Khorasan province, where baked bricks were used (YC·118 and 119). The reason for this could well have been of a defensive nature, as the two ice houses are located in an open countryside renowned for many raiders in the past[40]. Or perhaps baked bricks were used in this area because it was the norm for water reservoirs here (and in other regions). From a distance, the Amrani ice houses indeed looked like water reservoirs, but a closer inspection revealed typical ice house features. It is a sad fact that the adjoining Amrani

Fortress, built of mud materials and nowadays looking like a ghost town, has not resisted the elements and is crumbling fast (Fig. 5.67).

Fig. 7.12. YC-81 Jaffarabad

Dome interior shells

As for the visible inner shells, the mud brick surfaces were sometimes quite crude, but most often just straightforward corbelled surfaces. However, in some cases the masonry was made with decorative courses or patterns (Fig. 7.13). This raises a number of questions:

- Were the dome shells always made with horizontal brick courses, which gave the corbelled surface observed in most domes? Or were in some cases the mud-bricks inclined so that the sides of the bricks were flush with the finished shell surface?
- Was there a correlation between type of ice house and decoration, in the various provinces, or in villages, or at caravansaries?
- And why were the shells decorated when there was no access by the public to the interior?

Fig. 7.13 Dome interiors

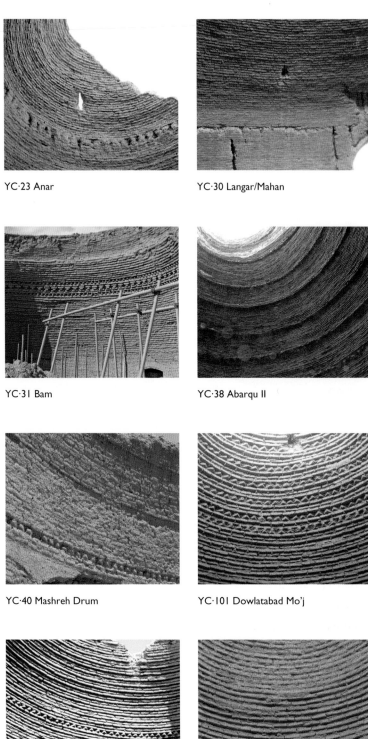

YC·23 Anar

YC·30 Langar/Mahan

YC·31 Bam

YC·38 Abarqu II

YC·40 Mashreh Drum

YC·101 Dowlatabad Mo'j

YC·108 Sabsevar I

YC·114 Soltanabad

In support of an analysis of these questions, the information in the table in Fig. 7.14 was extracted from the survey data from ice houses which could be accessed during the field work. The table records which ice houses had corbelled surfaces, which had flush surfaces and, in case of decoration, whether the interior decoration consisted in rows of fired bricks (which was also a reinforcement of the dome), courses of bricks turned horizontally, with the corner into the dome surface, bands of turned bricks at different levels, or by surfaces with different corbelling in successive courses. Under "remarks", the table records which ice houses had decorative parapets on the top of the shading walls or decorative patterns on the sides of the walls.

Fig. 7.13 and the data in the table (Fig. 7.14) allow the following conclusions or interpretations:

·   All accessed domed ice houses of the survey were built of corbelled mud brick courses. In the case of vertical inner shell surfaces (with no corbelling) the shell surface will be flush. Similarly, the greater surfaces of the large ice house domes (e.g. YC·34, 37, 38, and 39 in Yazd Province) will appear to be flush because the corbelling effect will appear negligible on a large surface in case of limited curvature. The field data and photographs similarly attest that all mud brick courses have been laid horizontally, not as courses spiraling towards the top of the domes.

·   Of the caravansary/fort ice houses,[41] only the ice house at the citadel of Bam (YC·31) had an interior decoration, which could be due to the citadel's prominence as an early residence for princes and governors, and as a staging post on the trade routes between India and the West since Sassanian times (Burke and Elliott 2008: 322). The other caravansary ice houses in Meybod/Yazd (YC·34), in Kashan (YC·42 and 43), at Dah Namak (YC·64 and 65), and at Abbasabad and Sadrabad (YC·106 and 107) had no such feature.

·   As for village ice house domes, the majority (40 nos.) had no decorations, 12 had various decorations or combinations of mud brick patterns. For the remaining ice houses, interior decorations could not be observed, but decorative parapets on the top of the shading walls or decorative patterns on the sides of the walls could be seen. A few domes (7 nos.) had wood elements of various shapes in them, see later for this aspect.

YC·No.	Corbelled surface	Dome not decorated	Rows of fired br.	Bands at diff. levels	Varied corbelling	Remarks
Tehran province						© for carav./fort
10	v	v				
12	v		v			
13	v	v				
Markazi province						
20	v					
Kerman province						
21	v					Dec. parapet
23	v					Row of wood
24	v					Dec. shad. wall
25	v	v				
26	v	v				Dec. parapet
27						Wall+parapet
28						Dec. parapet
30	v	v				
31©	v			v	v	8 courses
32						Wall+parapet
33	v	v				
Yazd province						
34©	v	v				Dec. parapet
37	v		v			
38	v		v			
39	v	v				Row of wood
Isfahan province						
40	v		v	v	v	
42©	v	v				
43©	v	v				
45	v	v				
Semnan Province						
55	v	v				
56	v	v				
57	v	v				
59	v	v				
60	v	v				
62	v	v				
63	v	v				
64©	v	v				

Fig. 7.14A. Dome interior decorations

One can understand why some of the shading walls had decorative parapets or patterns on the walls, as that would signify wealth and position of the ice house owner(s) to the outside, and maybe demonstrate the skills of the builder as well. And it would upgrade what is usually considered to be just simple rural architecture. But why put decorations inside the domes when they were invisible to the public? There could be a number of reasons:

YC·No.	Corbelled surface	Dome not decorated	Rows of fired br.	Bands at diff. levels	Varied corbelling	Remarks
65©	v	v				
73	v	v				
74	v				v	Top 4 meters
75	v					Row of wood
77	v	v				
78	v				v	
80	v	v				
81	v	v				
82	v	v				Wood grid at top
83	v	v				
88	v				v	Row of wood
89	v				v	
97	v				v	Wood in shell, 3 levels
98	v	v				
99	v	v				Top 5m, diff layers
100	v	v				Wood in shell, 3 levels
101	v			v	v	
103	v	v				Wood stumps
104	v	v				
105	v	v				
106©	v	v				Lots of wood
107©	v	v				
Razavi Khorasan province						
108	v		v	v	v	
109	v		v	v		Wood stumps, 1 level
112	v	v				Wood beams
113	v	v				
114	v		v	v		
115	v	v				Wood, 3 levels
116	v	v				Wood stumps
South Khorasan province						
123	v	v				
124	v	v				
126	v	v				
127	v	v				
128	v	v				

Fig. 7.14B. Dome interior decorations (continued)

· Persians appreciate art and decoration, and as a matter of course therefore decorate in an artistic manner utility structures like wind-catchers and pigeon-towers, so why not the tall, impressive ice house domes and walls, although the mud-plastered sloping outer surfaces of the ice house domes are impossible to keep decorated in the harsh climate?

· A nicely decorated interior of an ice house would bestow prestige on the owner of the ice house and its builder, who would thereby define a precedent and a standard other builders could not meet.

In modern terms a decorated interior would increase "the barrier of entry" for competitors, the builder would brand himself and be better placed for the next job in the next village. Both the owner(s) and the builder would be able to boast about and show – on demand only - their achievement to the outside world.

- A religious angle to the ice house decorations cannot be excluded as some of the patterns observed during the survey could resemble patterns on tiles in mosques or madressehs. Local contacts at Abarqu told me that the local mullah opened the parties, which were held when the ice house was full and was sealed, and again in summer when the ice house was opened for supply of ice to the community.

- Other reasons for the interior decorations have been considered – like fertility symbols, superstition or better acoustics – but have been discarded.

Wood inserts and reinforcements

The table in Fig. 7.14 – Domed interior decorations - conveys an impression of where wooden elements were found in the domes inspected during the field work, although wood is not considered a decorative element.

Due to the general scarcity of wood, ice houses were constructed in a manner to avoid its use; there was no evidence for the use of wooden beams or girders, or for scaffolding and supports during construction. Nevertheless, timber was found in a number of dome structures, and Fig. 7.15 shows a selection of domes with various forms of built-in wood elements. The wood is believed to have served one or more of the following purposes:

- Reinforcement of the dome by inserting flexible elements into the structure (against earthquakes?). This possibility appears very reasonable as the insertion of a flexible element in a rigid structure increases its resistance to particularly dynamic forces. But wooden pieces could also have served as tension reinforcement in case of large swelling or shrinkage after rainfalls.

- Creation of points of support for maintenance personnel during repairs. This reason appears inappropriate as the inner shell usually needed no maintenance.

Fig. 7.15. Wood elements

YC·75 Firouzabad

YC·82 Shamsabad

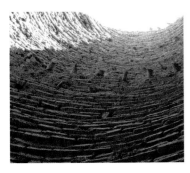

YC·88 Behdasht

YC·97 Biar Djamand

YC·103 Bostam

YC·106 Abbasabad

YC·109 Sabsevar II

YC·112 Ardoghesh

- Beams or purlins for suspending foodstuff or drinks for cooling in the open space above the ice pit. In Western Europe, meat and other foodstuff were often suspended from beams high over the floor. But the European ice houses did not feature an earthen pit in which the ice was stored and subsequently covered; in the west the entire building interior as such was an ice storage space. So, in Iran, such beams are assumed to have been solely a kind of reinforcement of the dome.
- Decoration or demonstration of wealth, as wood was scarce.

It is not possible to see a pattern in the use and placing of wood inserts in the Iranian ice house domes. Out of seven caravansary domes inspected, only one (YC·106 Abbasabad, between Sharud and Sabzevar) had wood inside the dome, both as wood stumps sticking out of the wall and as large cross beams four meters from the top. The wood elements in this case evidently served as reinforcement of the dome.

For the village ice house domes the use of wood varied from place to place. Occationally there was a single line of wood stumps in mud mortar instead of a mud brick course (YC·23, 39, 75, 88, and 109), and sometimes up to three layers (YC·97). Sometimes the wood stumps were only visible on the inside (e.g. YC·75), and alternatively they protruded through the outside surface (e.g YC·103). The large Shamsabad ice house (YC·82) had a grill of wood beams at the top of the inside shell, which is believed to be typical for ice houses with a very large ventilation hole at the top. The grill would support a tarpaulin or similar protection placed on the top of the ice house prior to heavy rain showers, while at the same time constitute a structural reinforcement of the dome with such a large opening at the top.

As one can see, wood reinforcements are not used to a large extent – wood was simply a scarce commodity in the project area – but they were seen in the provinces of Kerman, Yazd, Semnan, and Razavi Khorasan, but not in Tehran, Isfahan and South Khorasan.

Fig. 7.15 on the previous page illustrates the variety of domes with wooden inserts of varying types.

Ice pits and ice-making ponds

The ice pits and the shallow ponds were dug out of the natural soil. The walls of the ice pits were most often left unprotected, although sometimes they could be lined with a stone layer. The depth of the ice pits varied between 5 and 8 metres, and the pit was usually provided with one or more internal staircases (the use of ladders was reported in the *Mirâs Farhangi* reports).

The base of the ice pits was only accessible in a very few cases during the survey, and in only two cases, at Firouzabad (YC·75) and Bam (YC·31), were the remains of a drainage system in the bottom of the ice pit recorded. In addition, Abbasabad (YC·24) was reported to once have had one (Hourcade 1994: 92). Indications are that in most instances the ice house operators relied on simple seepage into the subsoil of the melt water from the stored ice.

Many popular sources explain that ice for ice houses was brought from nearby mountains (e.g. www.spititus-temporis.com/culture-of -iran/persian.contributions-to-humanity). In these cases shading walls and ice-making ponds were not necessary. But indications are that ice imported in this manner often supplemented the ice made on the ice house site.

Ice-making ponds had usually a width of the order of six meters, which is confirmed by the fact that the distance between the shading walls at Abarqu and Sabzevar (YC·37 to 39 and 108 to 109) varied between 8 and 13 meters, measured on site and confirmed by Google Earth images. The contours of ice pond widths of about six meters can be seen in the photograph in Fig. 1.2.

A simple calculation illustrates the shading effect of the tall ice house walls as a function of the sun angle over the horizon (Fig. 7.16).

Sun angles during the year for the city of Tehran (Ghobadian 1998: 4), and the corresponding lengths (L = H/tan v) of the shade of an eight meter tall wall (H) in direction east-west, are:

Fig. 7.16. Shade lengths calculation

Iranian Month	Western Month (circa)	Max. Sun Angle (v)	Shade Length (L)
Tir	July	78 degrees	1.70 m
Mordad – Khordad	August – June	75 degrees	2.14 m
Sharivar – Ordibehesht	September – May	67 degrees	3.39 m
Mehr – Farvardin	October - April	55 degrees	5.59 m
Aban – Esfand	November – March	42 degrees	8.89 m
Azar – Bahman	December – February	35 degrees	11.43 m
Dey	January	31 degrees	13.33 m

This table (Fig. 7.16) sends two messages:

(i) During the three winter months of December, January and February the sun reaches a maximum angle of 35 degrees and an eight meter tall wall will cast a shade of 11.43 meters or longer. This means that an eight meter tall wall will keep an ice-making pond in constant shade of up to ten meters width, allowing for a one meter sidewalk between the wall and the pond. If the wall shaded an ice storage pit, this could be up to ten meters wide, and the pit would be kept in shade during its filling in the cold winter months (cf. photographs in Fig. 6.3 and Fig 7.18 on pp. 142 and 192).

(ii) However, an ice storage pit of a walled ice house cannot be kept in shade during the hot summer days when the ice is taken out of the storage pit in July. For several hours around midday the shade of the wall is too short (only about two meters in the middle of the day) to shield the work place from solar radiation. The many square holes in the W-type ice house walls at Isfahan and Kuhpayeh indicate that wooden supports were set up in summer to hold a temporary roof or tarpaulin-like cover to provide shade.

Hourcade reported that in the Kerman area the sides of the shallow ice ponds were lined with baked bricks, while the base was natural soil (1994: 94). None of this could be confirmed during the survey as all water-related installations had vanished.

Ice production

General

As explained earlier, in-situ ice production took place in open-air shallow basins, in which water was frozen in successive layers. The thickness of such layers varied allegedly between 5 and 10 centimeters. In order to obtain an idea of the time required for the production of ice in the ponds, and of the time required to fill the ice-pit, I have used basic data on ice formation in sweet water lakes (EBr 1982 Vol. 9:166). The temperature of the water in a lake (and in my case, an ice-making pond or basin) falls mainly due to heat loss from the surface. This heat exchange occurs by (a) convection of air; (b) absorption, reflection and emission of long wave (thermal, infra-red) radiation; (c) absorption and/or reflection of short wave (solar) radiation; (d) evaporation.

(a) The most important factor for freezing water in an open-air pond is the convection of sub-zero temperature atmospheric air. The table below (Fig. 7.17) indicates the times required for ice sheet formation as a function of the sheet thickness and the ambient temperature. The column for minus four degrees below zero has been interpolated and added by me to enable comparisons with the number of days per year with sub zero temperatures for the weather stations in the Project Area, cf. table in Fig. 3.2 on page 31.

Layer Thickness	Air Temperature				
cm	~ 1 C	~4 C	~5 C	~ 10 C	~ 20 C
1	1.9 h	0.6 h	0.4 h	0.2 h	0.1 h
2	7.6 h	1.7 h	1.5 h	0.8 h	0.4 h
5	48 h	11.5 h	9.5 h	4.8 h	2.4 h
10	270 h	50 h	38 h	19 h	9.5 h

Fig. 7.17. Freezing times for sweet water (after EBr 1982 Vol. 9:166)

To take an example, a 2 centimeter, zero degree calm water depth takes 7.6 hours to freeze to ice at minus one degree atmosphere temperature. It takes only 1.7 hours if the temperature is (constantly or average) minus four degrees. And should the air temperature be ten degrees below zero, the freezing time will be only 0.8 hours.

It takes 11.5 hours to freeze a water layer thickness of 5 centimeters at an average air temperature of minus four degrees, i.e. in practice more than one night would be required. With an average air temperature of just minus one degree, 48 hours would be required, i.e. about a week of successive frost nights.

Water layers of 10 centimeters are hard to freeze, as they would need about a week of substantial frost (colder than minus four degrees every night and no thawing during the day) to succeed.

(b) Through clear sky, dry atmosphere and great altitudes, as found on the Iranian Plateau, infra-red (thermal) radiation into space will cause freezing of shallow water layers, even if the atmosphere temperature is not sub-zero. It has been reported that on cloudless nights in deserts the heat loss by radiation often was sufficient to freeze the water, even when the air temperature had not quite reached freezing (Clarke 1980: 206). Beazley describes a method practiced by the East India Company in the 18th and 19th centuries whereby ice was made in small unglazed earthenware pans under the open sky at night without frost (Beazley, E., and M. Harverson 1982: 55). A school mate of mine who lives in Saratoga, California, after having heard about my ice house project, wrote to me in August 2008 that he had himself made ice at night at near-zero temperatures in glazed clay pans, 35 centimeters diameter and 6 centimeters deep, placed in open country away from trees. Incidentally, my friend remembered that as a boy he witnessed ice blocks being cut out of the Esrum Lake and stored in the ice house of the royal castle of Fredensborg, north of Copenhagen, Denmark.

The effect of heat radiation into space is therefore not negligible. If one (conservatively) assumes that the net outgoing thermal radiation is 100 Watt per m[2] of water surface, the freezing of one millimeter of near-zero temperature water would take one hour, and two millimeters would take two hours (My thanks for the underlying analysis go to Associate Professor Aksel Walloe Hansen, of the University of Copenhagen, who, however, stresses the significance of the input assumptions, particularly about the radiation rate).

When applied to the table under section (a) above, the effect of thermal radiation would add almost 40 % to the effect of freezing by air convection at minus one degree Celsius, i.e. 2.76 centimeters instead of 2 centimeters would freeze in 7.6 hours. Therefore, the radiation effect enhances the "normal" freezing procedure, provided that the sky is clear, the air is dry, there is no wind to create a stir, and no snow on the ice surface to obstruct radiation. The effect of thermal radiation means that for a water layer of 5 centimeters the freezing time at minus four degrees would be of the order of 8-9, rather than 11.5, hours. Consequently the freezing of 5 centimeters per winter night appears possible, while the freezing of 10 centimeters is not possible at all at the prevailing frost degrees. These considerations imply that water layers of 5 centimeters or less would be the thickness used in ice house practice, which was confirmed by local informants.

(c) During daytime, the heating effect of solar radiation may thaw some ice, but this effect is mitigated by means of tall shading walls on the south side of the ice-making ponds at many ice house sites. Some ice houses had no shading walls at their ponds, and sunshine during the day would have resulted in some thawing of ice, unless the ponds were covered or shaded by other means during the day.

(d) Evaporation from the ice-making ponds extracts heat from the water. However, this effect is probably not of great importance, except that it could compensate for heating by solar radiation, as just noted in section (c), and for a greater air temperature during the day (noted in section (a)). The difference in temperature between night and day may well be in the order of twenty degrees (Siroux 1949:131).

Finally, snow on the open air ice ponds hinders freezing, partly due to its insulating effect towards the sky, partly because the snow would melt the ice if it melted during the day's sunshine. Snow was usually swept away immediately after snowfalls.

A calculation example

The ice house of Abarqu II (YC·38) is a good example for a quantification of the ice-making process. Local contacts (Messrs. Hamid M, Hossein H) indicated that filling of the ice houses took about two months.

Fig. 7.18. Ice production times

Assumption: Ice-making takes ca. two months, say a net of	50 days
Required ice thickness (2 batches, each 50 cm)	100 cm
I.E. required ice thickness production per day	2 cm
Table in fig. 7.17:	
Required temperature for 2 cm: minus one degree for 7.6 hours	
Table in fig. 5:	
Average annual number of days with below zero temp.:	91 days
Average annual number of days with below minus four:	43 days
Interpolation: Number of days with below minus one:	84 days
I.E. there are expected 84 days/year to cover the 50 days required	

It appears reasonable that the operators of the Abarqu II ice house could produce two batches of ice and thereby fill up the ice house within the winter season. With an expected average 84 days to cover the required 50, there is ample margin to cover years with less than average number of frost days.

The above calculation example allows a number of interpretations:

- If only one batch of ice were required, then only half the number of frost days would be required, i.e. 25 days, to produce the ice in the ponds. With the same safety margin and interpolation as for the Abarqu II case, the average annual number of frost days should be about 45 (25 x 84/50) to secure production on any site.
- When applying the limit of 45 days, it becomes clear from the table in Fig. 3.2 on page 31 that ice can be produced on sites across the major part of the Project Area, yet with some difficulty at Ardestan, Bafgh, Kashmar, Saveh, and not at all at Bam.
- The possibility of making two batches of ice exists at Abadeh, Abarqu (as we have seen), Biarjamand, Isfahan (including Kabutarabad), Kerman, Nishabur, Shahr-e-Babak, Shahreza, Shahrud, and Torbateh Heydarieh.[42]

These conclusions may be encumbered with some uncertainty, partly because the meteorological stations are not always located close to the ice houses in a particular area, and partly because there are in Iran a lot of locations with micro-climates that change over short distances. Still, despite the inherent uncertainly, the interpretation results appear reasonable and probable.

Operation

Domed ice houses

My contact, Mostafa S from Damghan, hand-wrote for me the following account of the operating procedure for a domed ice house with ice-making plant (DVP). Mostafa is deeply involved in cultural initiatives, and his account, collected from sources locally available in the Damghan area, appears to me more correct and complete than accounts obtained from sources such as Chardin (1927), Ferrier 1996), Rutstein and Kroll (1980), Zanger (2004), Burke and Elliott (2008), GN - *Ganjnameh* (2005), etc.:

"Ice houses are one of the inventions that were built mainly in the dry and hot areas on the fringe of the desert, with the purpose of covering the population's need for ice during the summer months. In terms of architecture and construction the ice houses were made of unbaked bricks, and their appearance was that of a conical dome. The dome had, from ground level to its top, several steps or stairs. The height of the dome varied between 10 and 15 meters. Inside the ice house building there was a deep pit, with its walls and bottom also made up of earth, a reversed cone shaped excavation which was used for the storage of ice. Outside and near the ice house there was situated a large open, rectangular basin (or several). In order to produce ice the ice house owners led water during the coldest months of the year into these basins (ponds) that had a depth of 40 to 50 centimeters. The water then froze into ice due to the low atmospheric air temperature. During frost nights the workers constantly sprinkled water onto the ice in the pond so that it froze and the ice layer became thicker and thicker. The surface of the ice was constantly raked and scratched by means of wood or metal tools so that the in-flowing water constantly froze. The ice thickness thus gradually grew to a maximum thickness of 50 centimeters. It was subsequently cut up into large blocks, which were moved to the ice house with special-made hooks. The ice blocks were slid down through the doorway of the dome. To avoid that the ice blocks got muddy, or froze together, straw and hay were placed in the doorway, along the bottom and the wall of the storage pit, and between the ice blocks. The process of producing ice and filling it into the storage pit continued during winter until the storage pit was filled up. Thereafter the doorway was closed by means of mud bricks and mud mortar in order to keep the inside of the dome cold.

It is important to note that the ice ponds were usually placed near the ice house. In order to expedite the freezing of water in the ponds they were situated close to the north side of high walls which shielded against wind and precipitation in general, and against the sun rays during daytime. In this manner, the temperature of the ice ponds remained lower than the surroundings, and the water froze to ice more quickly than would otherwise be the case.

Those ice houses that were situated near the township of Damghan and outside were all of the type of dome-shaped ice houses as described above. In this sort of ice houses there was usually at the bottom of the ice storage pit a cone-shaped hole and drainage channel so that melt water could be led away for use as irrigation water for the fields. Inside the dome wall, around the ice storage pit, there was usually a platform or *ramp for the traffic into and out of the ice house. Beyond the platform was then the thick wall of the ice house dome. The domes were usually built of unbaked mud bricks. For better protection and strength of the dome, and in order to minimize the building cost and the weight of the dome, the thickness of the dome wall was gradually reduced with height.*

The incredible height of the ice houses, 10 to 15 meters, was designed to keep the heat inside the dome high up and leave the lower part of the dome inside cooler. The use of straw or rash or other organic material between the ice blocks served to insulate and separate, and to secure that the stored ice blocks remained moist and protected when ice was taken out of the storage.

In short, in summer when the heat increased, the ice house owners opened up the ice house doors and delivered ice to the customers. After having sold the ice, and having covered their expenses, they shared the revenue amongst themselves. The inhabitants of the town and villages used most of the ice to cool their drinking water, and in later years before the introduction of electricity and refrigerators they used ice for making ice-cream."

In his description Mostafa S left out one important piece of information: There was a big party when the ice house was full at the end of the winter and sealed, and another big party took place when it was opened in the summertime. My Abarqu friends still remember the parties from their childhood.

People I met at the village of Hassan Khordu, near Mashad, told me that, during clear frost nights, water was diverted into shallow ponds in the open field and the ice was subsequently skimmed off in thin layers and packed down hard in the ice pit. This statement confirms that ice could be made without shading walls at the ice-making ponds. In typological terms this means that a DVO – domed village ice house with no ice-making plant – could have had in-situ ice-making. As confirmation, Siroux reports of places (Kashan and Varamin) where the cold is short and sharp and ice pools, unprotected by walls, were spread over several hectares (Beazley, E., and M. Harverson 1982: 54).

Walled ice houses

For walled ice houses, which were common in the Isfahan area, the web page of the Isfahan Municipality gives the following description (www.isfahan.ir):

"Ice, or rather ice blocks, has for many years been produced by tradition-al means in Isfahan. It is interesting to know how the ice was produced.
Traditional Ice Production
At first a large plot of several hectares of land was selected. On this land several shallow basins were dug out, so-called "beds" (kart), their size 50x20 metres, depth about 50 centimetres. At the end of autumn or the beginning of winter, when the weather became cold, water was led from streams or sources into the basins at evening time so that it could freeze into ice. Successively workers poured more water over the ice so that it became thicker and thicker.

At the entire south side of these basins thick walls of clayey soil or mortar were built, up to a height sometimes more than 10 metres. Sepa-rately, at a nearby location, a deeper hole was dug out, with a size of 30x6 metres and a depth of about 2 metres. A ramp or flight of steps was built into the pit, and the bottom of the pit covered by rush mats or straw.

By means of pickaxes or similar tools workers broke the ice in the basins into pieces or bars and carried them into the deep pit. This pro-cess continued over a period until the storage pit was filled up. The ice was then covered by rush mats, straw and soil so that the rays of the sun and the hot outside air could not penetrate down to the ice and melt it. In this way, the ice was conserved for several months until the summer season. At that time, the ice storage owners began the sale of the ice. For this purpose handcarts or donkey carts were made ready for the workers, who collected the ice from the storage side via the ramp or the stairs.

The exact number of such ice houses (ice plants) is not known, but each town district had usually one or two, depending on the population. Most of the ice houses were named after the town district they were in, or after the owner of the ice house.

According to the book "Half the World, the Story of Isfahan" by Mo-hammad Mahdi Ben Mohammad-Reza Al-Isfahani (year unknown), the number of ice houses in Isfahan amounted to about 40. He also writes that the number was higher in the past.

The traditional method for the making and the direct use of ice has not been hygienic, as contamination could come from both the source water and the insulating materials in the form of mats, straw or soil. But it was a cheap way of ice procurement and with no pollution unless the ice was used directly in drinking water or food.

With the advent of industrial ice production in large plants, using piped water, the pollution problem has largely been solved, and the use of ice has increased year by year ever since."

Fig. 7.18. Laborers at work in an ice pit

Already in the 17th century, the French traveller Thevenot reported about what seems to have been a walled ice house. According to his description, the ice was stored in a long trench along the north side of a wall, the trench was three fathoms deep and three to four feet wide, and the trench did not seem to be roofed with mud brick. The ice in storage, a fathom and a half deep, was covered with two to three feet of straw and reeds, and probably earth on the top. When with time the ice trench was no longer used, it was filled up with earth and the only visible remains would be the tall wall (Lovell 1687: 96).

When, in June 2007, I looked through a number of manuscripts in the library of the Shahid Beheshti University Architectural School, in Tehran, I found and copied the old photograph shown in Fig. 7.18. Its origin is uncertain, but the word "Tehran" is written on the frame. It shows workers in an ice storage pit of a walled ice house. They are raking and smoothing the surface in preparation for a new layer of ice for storage. It can be seen that the ice pit is a simple, unlined trench dug into the natural soil. In the background can be seen the wall of another ice house. When filling the ice pit, it was important to pack the ice as densely as possible because the loss by melting takes place from the ice surface – which consequently should be kept at a minimum.

The large town ice houses were commercial enterprises in which the ice was split up in quality groups according to purity, and sold at the gate, delivered to small butchers, dairies, etc., or distributed by street vendors (I remember that in the 1960s ice was sold from donkeys in the streets of Tehran, and there were strict warnings from fellow expatriates against consuming the ice, as it was usually infected with bacteria).

Underground ice houses

In his book on the climatic analysis of traditional Iranian buildings, Ghobadian reported on an underground ice house in Saveh, situated close to the Jozaghi Garden (*Bâgh-e-Jozaghi*). He showed a couple of photographs of a baked brick cellar dome and a door, both of which resemble the same features at the Taghrud ice house (YC·18), situated in the countryside 20 kilometers from Saveh in the direction of Qom. Extensive inquiries in Saveh revealed that there is not anymore an ice house in town. What is left is a drawing of the former Saveh ice house (Ghobadian 1998: 327), shown in Fig. 7.19. It has four sections of about 4 by 6 meters, partly buried under ground. The ice for storage is brought in from the high ground level (left side in the drawing), and it is later delivered to customers from the door visible in the foreground. The storage volume is estimated to be in the order of 500 cubic meters.

Like at Taghrud, the ice house, cellar and vaults were built of baked bricks, bonded by a mortar of fine sand, burned lime and ash. As already noted, the ice house had a door –on the left side on the drawing - for receiving the ice from the production sites outside town, or from the mountains. The ice was crushed into small pieces and water was poured over them to make a solid ice mass. In this type of cellar ice house, the ice was allegedly never covered with isolation materials like straw, reeds and earth (Ghobadian 1998: 327). During the summer, the ice house manager delivered ice from the lower door to the customers. In the homes, the ice was kept in insulated boxes and could last 4-5 days. In the houses in Tehran, the ice lumps were kept close to the tap at the bottom of the water reservoir where the temperature often was 10 degrees lower than outside (Ghobadian 1998: 327).

Fig. 7.19. Drawing of former Saveh town ice house (Ghobadian 1994:327)

Ice house employees

Mirâs Farhangi (1999) reports that the persons working at an ice house included: *Yakhchâli*: foreman, owner, lessor; *Yakhchâlbâ*: a person who guarded and protected the property; *Yakhchâldâr*: a person who produced ice, handled the water supply and ice movement. In the Kashan area it was recorded that a single, salaried official often had the responsibility for the three major service buildings of the village community – the mosque, the water reservoir and the ice house.

Ice distribution and use

An Englishman, Dr. C.J. Wills, who worked with the Indo-European Telegraph Department in 1866-81, was struck by the ready availability of ice: "*A great thing in such a warm place as Shiraz is the cheapness of ice; for about fifteen shillings in dear years and five in cheap ones, ice can be obtained all through the warm weather… A huge block is thrown in one's doorway each morning by the ice seller… So common is the use of ice that the poorest are enabled to have it, a big bit being sold for a farthing, and even the bowls of water for gratuitous drinking at the shop doors are cooled by it*" (Beazley, E., and M. Harverson 1982: 50).

The *Mirâs Farhangi* (1999) reports quote a National Geographic contributor (Samuel Matthews, year unknown): "*Even the poorest people had access to ice. The price depended on the purity and the use of the ice. Ice with soil and wood splinters – the lowest quality - was used for indirect cooling, i.e. it was put in a container before use as a cooling medium. A better quality was sold to the butcher. The best quality (bolouri/crystallic or shishe'i/glassy) was sold to households for the making of drinks. The quality was obviously reflected in the sales price. The ice was sold in qavar units (ca. 300 kilogrammes), price 18 sous. The ice was delivered in 60 livres portions (30 kilogrammes)"*.

Fryer (in Beazley, E., and M. Harverson 1982: 49) recorded of his stay in Shiraz, and later in Isfahan: "*They mightily covet cool Things to the Palat wherefore they mix Snow or dissolve Ice in their Water, Wine or Sherbets . . . The Poor they have but a Penny in the World, the one half will go for Bread and dried Grapes, or Buttermilk, and the other for Snow and Tobacco…*" (Fryer 1912: 249).

During the summer months the ice house staff took out every day the quantities needed by the entitled persons and customers. The ice was handed out in small blocks in particular containers or bags, which ensured the coolness of the ice during the short transport to the user.

In the villages, the ice was handed out on a daily basis to owners and workers, and the rest of the day's ration to others ("the poor"). There was usually no money involved. My Abarqu friend, Mehdi Houshmand, remembers how, as a boy in the 1950s, he carried the daily ice lump allocated to his family as a precious diamond back to his parents' house.

In the hot season, the ice was evidently used to cool drinks, but it was also turned into a wide gamut of sorbets and water ices flavored with pomegranate or rose, and whose reputation was legendary (Porter Y., and A. Thevenart 2003: 33).

8 | Status today - preservation

Opposite page
YC·123 Amirabad Sheivani

It is a sad fact that ice houses and other important remains of the Iranian utilitarian past disappear because they do not receive high enough priority by the Iranian people and the authorities. Ideally, examples of the large utilitarian structures should be re-established and re-used in order to demonstrate how organic industrial activity was exerted before the use of fossil fuels, and before concrete, steel and glass replaced soil as the prime construction material. No firm dates for when ice houses went out of operation were obtained, but the indications range from the late 1950s to mid-1970s (Hourcade 1994: 88). It was in the mid-1970s that the cultural heritage authorities first began to register ice houses in the provinces of Isfahan, Kerman, Tehran, and South Khorasan.

An important perspective at the outset of this project was whether the handsome and valuable ice house architecture of Iran would be remembered and preserved, or whether it would be "restored" and kept as a few specimen of dubious value. As my documentation and photographs demonstrate, the majority of the ice houses have disappeared. Wall and underground types decline first - and completely - because there appears to be little interest in the conservation of ice houses without domes. For domed ice houses the situation is better, but far from ideal: The domes at the ice houses YC·17 Koleyn, YC·20 Mehdiabad, YC·25 Kabutar Khan, YC·37 Abarqu I, YC·38 Abarqu II, YC·39 Abarqu III, YC·46 Zavareh (in progress), YC·64 Dah Namak, and YC·116 Khaf (in progress) have largely been restored. And, for the ice houses YC·21 Ravar, YC·24 Rafsanjan, YC·26 Moayeri Kerman, YC·27 Rigabad Kerman, YC·28 Zarisf Kerman, YC·32 Sirjan, YC·34 Meybod, the restoration included the shading walls, fully or partly, but never any part of the system for water supply and ice-making.

In some places, only the street names remind us of once existent ice houses: Kucheh Mehr (Manucheri area, Tehran), Yakhchal alley in Isfahan, and Yakhchal Street (Gholhak suburb, Tehran). Or,

Fig. 8.1. Ice house re-use

YC·I Arbab Taghi

YC·7 Kan

YC·21 Ravar

YC·74 Maheleh Chup

YC·79 Forat

YC·85 Qaleh Agha Baba

YC·105 Miami

YC·110 Maidan Gusfand

Province	Year of first registration	First year with min. 5. registrations	Total no. of registrations	Year of first ice house registration	Total number of ice houses registration	No. of ice houses reg. in project	No. of ice houses localized in this project
East Azerbaijan	1931	1968	447				Outside
West Azerbaijan	1931	1965	322	1998	3	0	Outside
Ardebil	1931	1966	232				Outside
Isfahan	1931	1931	829	1975	2	2	14
Ilam	1931	2000	205				Outside
Bushehr	1931	1998	122				Outside
Tehran	1931	1955	685	1977	3	3	17
Ch. Mahal & Bakhtiari	1969	1999	214				Outside
North Khorasan	1967	1967	100				Outside
South Khorasan	1937	1977	342	1977	3	3	7
Razavi Khorasan	1931	1931	914	2001	11	8	15
Khuzestan	1931	1931	490				Outside
Zanjan	1931	1974	307				Outside
Semnan	1931	1931	407	2002	16	16	54
Sistan & Balouchest.	1931	1966	241				Outside
Fars	1931	1931	1028				Outside
Qazvin	1931	1976	1173				Outside
Qom	1931	1998	169				1
Kordestan	1939	1977	587				Outside
Kerman	1931	1966	352	1975	9	9	13
Kermanshah	1931	1931	625				Outside
Kahgilvieh	1937	1977	221				Outside
Golestan	1931	1967	385				Outside
Gilan	1938	1977	743				Outside
Lorestan	1931	1997	424				Outside
Mazanderan	1931	1931	366	2003	2	0	Outside
Markazi	1931	1975	241	2002	1	1	2
Hormozegan	1973	1975	115				Outside
Hamedan	1931	1931	373	2000	1	0	Outside
Yazd	1933	1967	642	1996	5	5	6
Total			13301		56	47	129

Fig. 8.2. Highlights of national registration of ice houses (situation in 2005)

in a few cases, parts of restored ice houses (domes and sometimes fragments of walls) have been incorporated into public parks. In other cases, the high quality of the mud brick work in ice houses is demonstrated by their conversion into garages, restaurants, ammunition dumps, goat stables, etc. Of the walled ice houses, only one is in (converted) use today as a mechanic's workshop, in the Tehran suburb of Kan, see Fig. 6.2 and Fig. 8.1.

The book *Iranian Artifacts Registered in the List of National Monuments* (Pazooki and Shadmehr, 2005) contains 13,400 items registered up until 2005. Of this number, 6650 are buildings (371 water cisterns, 68 fire temples, 66 mills, 1083 mausoleums, 63 gardens, 49 dams and weirs, 135 bazaars, 226 bridges, 164 hoseiniehs, 9 convents, 108 towers of silence, 31 villas and mansions, 33 gates, 1 observatory, 77 churches, 345 baths, 651 castles and forts, 132 palaces, 349 caravansaries, 45 minarets, 152 schools, 739 mosques, 61wash houses, and 56 ice houses). 6967 items in another group are mounds (5836), collections (1064), and fabrics (67). Finally, there is a group of 785 items, which include squares (13), caves (129), cemeteries (317), qanats (25), inscriptions (38), reliefs (68), and miscellaneous (195). All these numbers are encumbered with a small uncertainty as my sums do not exactly match those of the National Registry (NR).

The table in Fig. 8.2 contains an overview of the numbers and dates of registration in the Iranian provinces up to 2005, with an emphasis on ice houses:

- Formal registration of Iranian national cultural heritage began in 1931 in 22 of the 30 provinces and was then gradually initiated in the remaining provinces up to as late as 1973; the latest was Hormozegan Province, around Bandar Abbas. The French archaeologist André Godard became Head of the Archaeological Service in 1928 and one of his main tasks was to set up a national registration of artefacts.

- The largest group of registrations are mounds, which are followed in number by Islamic installations such as mosques, hosseiniehs, mausoleums, minarets, and cemeteries. Types of desert architecture are much rarer.

- The registration efforts developed swiftly in the provinces of Isfahan, Razavi Khorasan, Khuzestan, Semnan, Fars, Kerman, Kermanshah and Hamedan, as already a minimum of five registrations were made during the first year. In all other provinces the pace was much slower, as five registrations were only reached in the 1960s and 1970s; in the provinces of Ilam, Bushehr, Qom and Luristan, even as late as 1997 to 2000.

- The provinces with the highest number of registrations are Qazvin (1173) and Fars (1028). In the provinces within the Project Area the number of registrations are: Isfahan (829, of which 2 are ice houses), Tehran (685, of which 3 are ice houses), South Khorasan (342, of which 3 are ice houses), Razavi Khorasan (914, of which 8 ice houses are within the Project Area), Semnan (407, of which 16 are ice houses), Kerman (352, of which 9 are ice houses), and Yazd (642, of which 5 are ice houses). In total, 56 ice houses were included in the National Register in its 2005 edition of which 47 were situated in the Project Area.

- National registration of ice houses began comparatively late; in the provinces of Isfahan, Tehran, South Khorasan and Kerman in the mid-1970s, and in the provinces of Yazd, West Azerbaijan, Hamedan, Razavi Khorasan, Semnan, Markazi and Mazanderan only in the years 1996 to 2003.

· In spite of this late start, the provinces of Razavi Khorasan and Semnan had already reached 11 and 16 ice house registrations, respectively, in 2005. A visit to the *Mirâs Farhangi* office in Semnan revealed that at least six more ice houses will be included in the next NR edition, expected in 2010.

· With only 56 registrations in the NR, ice houses represent only 0.4 percent of the total, while water cisterns account for almost 3 percent. The average percentage of ice house registrations (47) in the provinces bordering the central deserts is higher, reaching 1.1 percent of all registrations in the area. But registration does not imply preservation.

The number of 129 ice houses identified during this project compares favorably with the official registration efforts – the number of registered ice houses has almost tripled – although probably several more ice houses could have been found. All registered ice houses that still exist are of the domed type, except for one, Rahimabad, in the town of Birjand (YC·125) and presumed to have been of the underground type.

Unfortunately, as noted, registration has not in general resulted in preservation and protection. While the province of Semnan deserves praise for its registration effort, not one of the registered ice houses there is being maintained and kept from deteriorating. The same goes for Isfahan and Razavi Khorasan Provinces, where only the dome at Khaf (YC·116) seemed to have been restored in 2008. Domes of NR-registered ice houses have also been repaired and restored in Tehran Province (YC·10 and YC·11), in Markazi Province (YC·20), in Kerman Province (YC·21, YC·24, YC·26, YC·28 and YC·32), and in Yazd Province (YC·34, YC·37 and YC·39). In a few instances, shading walls have been restored, but nowhere have former water ponds for ice-making and the associated water supply systems been included in the preservation effort.

As regards types other than domed ice houses, the situation is even bleaker. The walled ice houses in the Isfahan area and the Tehran suburb of Kan are all crumbling. The walls of the ice houses of Arbab Taghi (YC·1) in Tehran and Rahimabad (YC·125) in Birjand have been left in such a state that does not allow a firm assessment whether they originally belonged to a walled or an underground ice house.

Fig. 8.3. YC·34 Meybod ice house
under restoration

In writing about Yazd, Modarres (2006) illustrates how a nation, in the process of reconstituting a national identity in the image of its glory days, may unknowingly forget the importance of local identities and vernacular architecture. This is part of the reason why the preservation of ice houses, for instance, receives little attention. Modarres further shows that the destruction of vernacular architecture provides the "ruins" that other researchers considered as necessary instruments for reconstruction of an imagined past (2006: 5). The pendulum swings between varying degrees of preservation of monumental and vernacular architecture while trying to establish a national cultural identity, which is being eroded at the same time (ibid). Old adobe buildings, coffee houses, and passion plays appear to be the embarrassing symbols of a feudal, pre-modern existence. Although many people know the value of vernacular architecture, they have no resources to stop the flow of asphalt and concrete. The

loss of vernacular architecture amounts to losing the soul of a neighborhood (2006: 159). According to Modarres (2006: 167), there are many explanations for why old buildings are not preserved:

Fig 8.4. YC-27 Rigabad
view from northeast

- lack of funding;
- weak perception of heritage by the general population;
- social opposition to a preservation agenda (which is sometimes seen as a minority elite agenda);
- assumptions regarding the efficiency of modern planning;
- absence of urban amenities (e.g. leisure and entertainment facilities) in the older neighborhoods;
- diminishing interest in the religious attractions of older neighborhoods.

Modarres' book paints a picture of the loss of place, neighbourhood and memory. Vernacular architecture creates a sense of place, yet there is an ongoing destruction of the delicate texture and scale of neighbourhoods, with their distinct features. The transformations are signs of economic success, but they erode the physical culture of a place. My own observations indicate that ice houses are often surrounded by mortal enemies. They will disappear – an element of human development will be gone – and the world will be poorer for it.

So, restoration and preservation does sporadically take place, with mixed results. Three examples are offered here:

a) The old photograph of the Meybod Ice House (YC·34, Fig. 8.3), photographed by me at the Water Museum in Yazd, conveys an impression of the method and extent of its restoration, which took place in the late 1990s. It appears that the original ice house surface had steps of one meter height, which, together with the external stairs on the north side, allowed access to the entire surface for maintenance and repair of the *kâh-gel* surfacing. The restoration does not restore the steps (!), for which reason it becomes necessary to build up a scaffold for access. The external restoration of the dome takes place from the top and down, a procedure that can only be used when the outer layer is peeled off. One observes, then, that the restoration is not faithful, neither to the construction method, as the ice house originally was built without the use of a scaffold or support, nor to the original shape, as the restored dome received a smooth surface, as can be seen today. The ice houses at Zavareh (YC·46) and Khaf (YC·116) were in the process of restoration in the same manner as that of Meybod.

b) The Rigabad in Kerman (YC·27) presents itself today as a nicely restored domed ice house with a decorated western shade wall, but with no trace of the water supply system, and no trace of an eastern shade wall it once had.

In the 1970 aerial photo in Fig. 8.5 it is seen that the Rigabad ice house once had two curved shade walls, towards both west and east. However, the recent photos show that the eastern shade wall had been demolished and removed to give way to a new boulevard. There is no indication on the site, or elsewhere, that the ice house installation has been seriously amputated (Fig. 5.15).

c) The ice house at the Citadel of Bam (YC·31) is a special case (Fig. 8.6). During many years of neglect, the dome had collapsed and only the lower six meters remained standing. Concurrently with the restoration of the citadel, the ice house was restored and rebuilt with international aid in the years 1974 to about 2000. Due to the powerful earthquake on 26 December 2003,

Fig. 8.5. YC·27 Rigabad at Kerman, with two qanats. Aerial photo from c.1970 (Rainer 1977: 198)

the rebuilt dome collapsed once again, and during my visit in 2007 the ice house appeared as in the photographs in Figs. 8.6 and 8.7. At that time the debris and damaged parts of the wall had been cleared away. Together with the almost completely destroyed citadel – the largest mud brick building complex in the world – the ice house now awaits new decisions and funding for its reconstruction.

Fig. 8.6. YC·31 Bam ice house under restoration

In Fig. 8.7 I have combined two photographs in order to show the magnitude and grandeur of the Bam ice house in spite of the severe 2003 earthquake damage.

In summary, most ice houses will melt away because they are made of mud and mud bricks. In rare cases, attempts have been made to preserve some of the more spectacular elements – domes and to a lesser extent walls – but never any ice ponds or water channels. It somehow seems much easier to decide to preserve the principal cultural heritage from the distant past, from the more distant and aesthetically refined periods of history, than to save remains of the recent utilitarian past. A more proactive form of intervention and preservation is needed than just the "just freezing" or "just let it be" of certain function-empty time capsules. Ideally, the large utilitarian structures should be re-established and re-used to demonstrate how organic industrial activity was executed before the use of fossil fuels. A computer-animation of the reconstruction of an ice house could be another way of keeping the memory of the ice houses and their role alive.

Opposite page
Fig. 8.7. YC·31 Bam, on the way - again

9 | Summary and Conclusions

Opposite page
YC-25 Kabutar Khan

An ice house is an installation for storing ice blocks from winter for use in the summer. While ice houses have been well known in Europe for almost 400 years, they have been known in the Near East for over 3000 years. This book presents the results of a comprehensive field survey of the ice houses of the Iranian Central Plateau, and endeavors to answer the questions as to where, how, and why the ice houses were built, operated and largely forgotten. A total of 129 ice houses were documented during the survey.

I had seen examples of this eminent piece of vernacular and organic architecture some 50 years ago when I was building roads across the deserts in central and east Iran. The ice houses I saw all had a tall mud brick dome over a subterranean ice storage pit and one or several tall east-west running mud walls, which had protected as shading walls a number of open-air, shallow ice-making ponds. The last ice houses in Iran went out of use in the 1960s, when electricity and mechanical refrigeration supplanted them, and they have been left to decay and disappear.

Iran is famous for its rich cultural heritage, and a vast literature has been produced over the ages within the fields of archeology, architecture, art history and other cultural disciplines. Yet, very little has been written about ice houses, and no archaeological evidence for them before the 17th century AD has been found. Before the inception of this project, no focused and comprehensive study of the Iranian ice houses had ever been carried out. Clearly there was a need to do something about this grave deficiency.

The Project Area is situated in and below the piedmont zone of the mountain ranges on the alluvial fans and plains that surround the central deserts, Dasht-e-Lut and Kavir-e-Lut. The demand for ice houses is determined by the intense heat of this region; the Iranian Plateau is one of the hottest and driest areas in the world. Ice could only be made there if the winters were very cold, with frost, and if there were available water and suitable building ma-

SUMMARY AND CONCLUSIONS 209

terials for the ice storage houses. These conditions are met on the Iranian Plateau, which displays a hot and dry continental climate. Water is provided by the ingenious qanat system, which made living on the desert rim possible; and in large parts of these areas the clayey soils are suited for both irrigated agriculture and as building material.

Qanats (*qanât*) are subterranean conduits that tap the ground water-bearing soil layers near the mountains and lead the water underground out into the alluvial plains near the deserts and thus made settlement and agriculture possible. Qanats were being utilized by the time of the Achaemenid Empire (6th – 4th centuries BC), and the Persians introduced the technique into Egypt after they conquered it in 525 BC. There is uncertainty about the time of the first qanats, which apparently originated in ancient Urartu (located in modern day western Iran, eastern Turkey, Armenia, and northern Iraq). Unfortunately, even greater uncertainty about the origin of the ice houses of Iran prevails. But it is suggested here that their invention and development are intimately linked with the development and spread of qanat systems.

It was as late as in the 1970s before the Iranian cultural heritage authorities began to be interested in ice houses, and official registration began in the provinces of Isfahan, Tehran, South Khorasan and Kerman. Of the 56 ice houses in the National Register, 47 are located on the fringe of the large central deserts, i.e. in the Project Area.

Initial hypotheses for the present study were that a comprehensive inventory of Iran's ice houses had never been made; that a complete survey was probably not possible but worth a try; that Iran's ice houses all had tall clay domes over an ice pit, and large shade walls on the side; that they were organic inventions built by local people without the use of mechanical gear or support, and with local materials; that they were a rural phenomenon and typical for the Iranian Plateau; that they were located near settlements at least 60 years old when ice houses went out of use; and that they were a derivative of the qanat system and placed in relatively well-off rural communities.

Besides getting as much information as possible from the Iranian cultural authorities in Tehran and the provinces, the first step in preparation for the field work was to find available literature and other material about vernacular architecture, in particular ice houses, in order to better focus the subsequent search.

The field work took place in the years 2007 to 2009 and included 23,000 kilometers of travel throughout the Project Area. At all sites, the location was determined by GPS equipment, which furnished latitude, longitude and elevation above sea level. These x-y-z coordinates are unique and exact, while names of locations and villages may be encumbered with some uncertainty because many of them were communicated to me orally. During the entire project the field survey was supplemented by comprehensive studies of the published literature, internet sources, maps, satellite imagery, and aerial photographs purchased from the Iran Geographical Organization.

The ice house study has addressed the following questions:

(a) How many Iranian ice houses have survived, bearing in mind that they have gone out of use and were built of perishable mud materials? Considering the vast spaces involved, does an inventorying survey make sense?

(b) What is their distribution? Is there a pattern in their distribution relative to topography and other environmental factors, such as soils, water and climate?

(c) Is there a variation in types from the examples I saw forty years ago in the towns of Kerman, Sirjan and Abarqu?

(d) What factors contributed to their construction and operation?

(e) What was their function in their respective localities?

(f) Can their origins and history be traced?

(g) What is the status nowadays regarding the preservation of ice houses?

1. The main contributions of this study are summarized in the sections a-d below, concerning the survey results, distribution, variations in type, and the construction details of ice house domes:

a) The survey found, registered and mapped in total 129 ice house sites, of which remnants of ice houses were found on only 104 of them. This represents the main accomplishment of this project; the 86 newly registered ice houses almost triple the number of registered examples (4 of those on the National Registry could not be found). 104, of the 129, were located at villages and had served the rural population, 12 were located at caravansaries or forts, and 13 had served towns, including the metropolis of Tehran. 111 had (had) domes, 6 had been of a walled type, and 12 had (had) underground ice storage reservoirs. Of the total of 129 ice houses, 71 had (had) an associated open air ice-making plant, and 58 had (had) no ice-making and were pure ice storage facilities. The existence of a further 10 ice houses was indicated to me by reliable sources (the National Registry, appraisal reports of the Cultural Heritage Organization, literature references, or local contacts) but they could not be found and classified.

The main results of the field work, complemented by data such as registration number and age of artifact from the National Registry, are presented in the table in Figs. 4.3 A-C on pages 56-61, List of Ice Houses in the Project Area. A map with all identified ice house sites is found in Fig. 4.9 on page 68. The Ice House List is complemented by a 500-page Ice House Catalogue contained in the appendix of the original dissertation. Ice House Catalogue details are available from the author, on demand. The bulk of this book is a description of all registered ice houses that still exist in some form, sorted after province, shape, user category and availability of ice fabrication (pages 81 to 153).

As noted already, this project has added greatly to the number of registered ice houses in Iran. However, because of the vast spaces to be covered within the Project Area, the number probably remains incomplete. Still, this exercise has been worthwhile, based on the amount of new evidence and analyses produced.

b) The 129 registered ice house sites are situated in the following provinces: Tehran (17), Qom (1), Markazi (2), Kerman (13), Yazd (6), Isfahan (14), Semnan (54), Razavi Khorasan (15), and South Khorasan (7) (see the map in Fig. 4.7). Concentrations of ice houses were found in the countryside in the vicinity of the towns of Tehran (9 examples), Kerman (3), Abarqu (3), Isfahan (5), Garmsar (10), Semnan (4), Shahrud (5), Sabzevar (3), and Birjand (6).

The location of ice houses seems to be based primarily on the local climate, soil conditions, and the availability of water, or of natural ice in the nearby mountains, along with social factors in the form of demand and relative wealth of the community served by the ice houses. The apparent correlation between concentrations of ice houses and particular elevations thus appears to be irrelevant. The distribution of the dome type without ice-making plant (DVO) along the southern piedmont of the Elburz Mountains on a line from south of Tehran to Nishabur, and around Gonabad in the east, and the distribution of all the classical dome type with ice-making plant (DVP), with the exception of the Mahabad (YC.45) example, in the wide zone south and southeast of Kashan, including Yazd and Kerman Provinces, seem to corroborate these conclusions. This pattern is confirmed by the same distribution of the caravansary/fort ice house types. The few remaining examples of underground and wall types in the Tehran and Isfahan town areas, where local sources indicate that the number once was more than eighty and forty, respectively, is clearly due to urban sprawl, and at the same time the complete absence of interest for preservation of the industrial cultural heritage.

Distribution patterns revealed by the survey suggest the following: Domed ice houses probably were never used in towns, where walled or underground types prevailed. In fact, it may be concluded that all large commercial or industrial ice plants were of the latter types. The large underground ice houses in and near towns (i.e. Tehran) probably all had associated ice plants. On the other hand, no walled types served villages, and underground types seem to have been very rare here. Caravansaries and forts had only domed ice houses, probably because this type was compact, and easier to operate and defend than the other more open types.

In terms of environmental interface, all ice houses were found to be located on alluvial plains at altitudes varying between 830 meters above sea level in the western desert fringe and over 1800 meters in the Kerman area in the southern zone. No obvious pattern was found in the distribution of ice houses in relation to the soil quality, and the composition of the soils at the ice house sites themselves was found to be sandy clay. A comparison of the climatic conditions in the north along the Elburz Mountains with the large plains towards the south along the Zagros range show no difference in the average numbers of frost days per year, i.e. the potential for open-air ice-making is the same across the Project Area. The proximity of the large deserts at several ice house locations does not appear to have been a significant factor.

c) As I have emphasized in the body of the book, there did turn out to be both a variation in types and within types.

Domed ice houses: Dome shapes were paraboloid, i.e. with a parabola cross section, with varying combinations of heights and external diameters; on average the height was 72 per cent of the diameter, but great variations were observed, especially for those domes which were sitting on a cone-shaped plinth structure. All domes visited had visible corbelled mud brick shells inside, rarely with a thin plaster layer, in some cases with decorative brick courses. The domes often had stepped outer surfaces, which would enable access for maintenance without support gear. Smooth domes had one or more spiraling staircases for access. Domes generally had vent holes, which would enable the evacuation of the hot air at the top. Doors were usually placed at the east and west sides, only seldomly at the sunny south side.

The majority of domed ice houses had only one dome with one shading wall. But at Sirjan there were two, linked by a curved shading wall; at Birjand a set of twin ice houses was found 100 meters apart. At Sabzevar, the remains of two installations, each with three large domes, and with eight and eleven shading walls respectively, were seen.

For small groups of ice houses – in the areas of Garmsar, Damghan, Shahrud, Sabzevar and Birjand – similarities in style may indicate that the same (group of) builders had been at work. On the other hand, at Abarqu, where the survey registered three large ice houses with similar dimensions, the different designs may indicate different builders and/or different dates of construction.

Domed ice houses with ice-making facilities had one or more large shading walls on the south side of the ice ponds. Shading walls were usually 8 meters tall, which would create constant shade of a minimum of 10 meters during the winter months for ice-making ponds.

Walled ice houses: The wall type ice houses are of a very simple design, i.e. a long east-west rectangular storage pit, protected on the south, east and west sides by a tall wall providing shade and shelter. At none of the four sites visited was there any trace of the ice-freezing ponds and water channels, which were situated in large areas near the storage.

Underground ice houses: Like walled ice houses, underground ice houses are few and disappearing, and, in fact, remains of the storage cellars were found at only two sites. At one cellar, fired bricks had been used, and at the other the usual mud bricks.

It appeared that other ice house types than the ones described in this book may have existed in Iran, and that not only ice but also snow was used as a cooling medium. In addition, seven ice houses outside the Project Area were found and their position indicated as a basis for future research.

d) Dome Construction: With the exception of three baked brick ice houses in the east Iran province of South Khorasan, all ice house installations were built of mud, being either in the form of sun-dried mud bricks, plaster (*kâh-gel*) or so-called *sefteh* mortar, always with varying contents of straw or chaff as a kind of fiber reinforcement, along with *sefteh* foundation materials mixed with lime and sometimes stone temper.

The construction of domed ice houses follows more or less the same principle as for the better known water reservoirs (*âb-anbâr*), yet with a shallower and broader pit, dug in a funnel shape. The ice house in Fig. 7.1 represents the classical and most common configuration of the DVP/DCP type, which displays a dome with an attached east-west running, straight shading wall. There are slight variations to this layout: If a shading wall was not oriented east-west, then it was turned slightly clockwise to better protect against the afternoon sun; and a group of domed ice houses had several parallel shading walls.

The dome shapes for the 94 domed ice houses surveyed vary greatly within the spectrum between pure cones and paraboloids. The majority are termed paraboloids, some with tapered and others with straight surfaces, but not one particular shape could be judged to dominate. There also seems to have been no significant difference between the shape of ice house domes standing alone (DVO and DCO) and the shape of domes having associated shading walls for ice-making ponds (DVP and DCP). Optimally, the shape generally minimized the surface towards the sun and at the same time reached a certain height. The higher the dome, the better is the cooling effect at the bottom, due to what is called "the thermal piston", or the "thermal column". To ensure that no tension forces occur in the dome, the dome must have a certain thickness, and when the dome has a certain thickness and weight, variations of the ideal shape can be used without the danger of tension cracks and ruptures at the surface. None of the ice house domes had a spherical shape. Pointed domes importantly create height for better cooling, they obtain the best combination of strength and weight, and they minimize exposure to the sun in the middle of the day.

All village ice house domes surveyed were made of mud bricks set in mud mortar. For larger domes, the mud bricks were built up in two or even three brick-widths, which were subsequently plastered with mortar on the outside for weather protection. All accessed domed ice houses of the survey were built of corbelled horizontal mud brick courses. By building up first the inner dome shell by successive rings of mud bricks, with each successive ring only protruding a few centimeters from the preceding one, and with one or two more mud brick shells added to the outside of the inner shell, along with a mud mortar layer on the exterior, a stable mud structure in compression was maintained during the whole process. In addition, the exterior of the dome was shaped in a way to allow access without supports, or a set of stairs was cut into the surface for easy access.

2. Information concerning sections e) and f) was much more difficult to come by, yet I submit that I have made headway into both the role of ice houses in the social networks of villages and towns, and the thorny issue of the origins of ice houses in Iran:

e) These often spectacular examples of vernacular construction must have represented significant aspects of village architecture. It appears that private landlords, vaqfs, or cooperatives could own and operate the ice houses that were built in some of the near-desert villages in the Project Area. The festivities associated with the filling of the ice houses in the winter, and with their opening and the distribution/sale of ice in the summer, indicate the social importance of these institutions for some village societies in Iran in the recent past. The large town ice houses, on the other hand, were industrial enterprises, in which the ice was split up into types based on quality and sold to a variety of customers on a commercial basis, either at the gate of the ice house, or delivered to butchers, dairies, restaurants, etc., or sold in the streets.

f) Although it seems to me to be reasonable to connect the origin and history of these structures to that of the qanats, in the first millennium BC, there appears to be no textual or archaeological evidence for their existence in Iran before the 17th century AD. Domed structures existed already in the Bronze Age Near East and ice houses are mentioned as early as the Middle Bronze Age, although the latter seem to be simple ice storage units (cellars) in palatial buildings.

3. The future of these unique structures appears bleak:

g) National Registration does not translate into preservation. No ice house exists anymore in its original form and full extent. The domes of a few ice houses have been restored, and some shading walls have been repaired or restored to the original shape. However, the restoration of some domes, at least, does not follow the original shape or traditional building methods. There is no evidence that any part of the less spectacular aspects of ice houses - the water supply and the associated ice-making system – has been preserved or restored. And, it needs to be emphasized that already at twenty-five ice house sites – out of the 129 surveyed - all traces of the ice house installation have completely disappeared. Unless a concerted effort is made, the prognosis is not good for the majority of the rest.

Notes

1. An article "When fridges were as big as houses", in the newspaper Daily Telegraph on 05 August 2006, quotes an Elizabeth David who claims that the Greenwich ice house was a snow pit built in 1619 for King James I. At least 2,500 ice houses still existed in Britain in 2006, the article claims (www.telegraph.co.uk).
2. All photographs are by the author unless otherwise stated.
3. My investigations found the height to be 18 meters.
4. Local contact Mehdi H in February 2007.
5. Reference quoted from Beazley, E., and M. Harverson (1982: 49).
6. Reference taken from Porter and Thévenart (2003: 34).
7. The provinces of Azarbaijan, Hamadan, and Mazanderan – as well the northern part of Razavi Khorasan – are outside the Project Area.
8. The White Revolution comprised a combined six-point program including (1) land reform; (2) sale of government-owned factories to finance land reform; (3) a new election law including women's suffrage; (4) the nationalization of forests; (5) a national literacy corps; and (6) a plan to give workers a share of industrial profits (Keddie, N.R., and Y. Richard 2006: 145).
9. *"On the fourth day you come to a river of fresh water, but one which has its channel for the most part underground. In some parts, however, there are abrupt openings, caused by the force of the current, through which the stream becomes visible for a short space."* (Rugoff 1961: 71)
10. H. Kanter and P. Delougaz. *Chogha Mish, Vol.I, The First Five Seasons of Excavations 1961-1971*. Oriental Institute Publication 101, 1996. A. Alizadeh. *Chogha Mish, Vol. II, The Development of a Prehistoric Regional Center in Lowland Susiana, Southwestern Iran: Final Report on the Last Six Seasons of Excavations: 1972-1978.* Oriental Institute Publication 130, 2008.
11. Ice house identification numbers will be explained later.

12. In Western Europe, a 24-hour cycle with temperatures not under 20 degrees centigrade is termed "Tropical "(DSDE Vol.19 2001: 275).

13. 65/23 days means 65 frost days of which 23 have temperatures below minus four degrees centigrade.

14. Siroux, in his book on caravansaries and smaller roadside buildings in Iran, reported that the temperature difference between areas in the sun and in the shade could reach 15 to 20 degrees (1949: 131).

15. Comprehensive descriptions of qanât systems are found in Bonine (1982:145) and by Boucharlat (in Briant 2001: 158).

16. Repeated in Christensen (1993:129).

17. With archaeologists/historians Knoepfler, Chatelain, Wuttmann, Chauveau, Savini, Boucharlat, Bousquet, et al.

18. The description of qanat building is inspired by the writings of Beazley, E., and M. Harverson (1982: 34), Wulff (1966: 251), Smith 1966: 82), and Bonine (1982: 145). See also Wulff's article in *Scientific American* (April 1968: 94-105).

19. Qanat gradients are of the order of 1/1000. They can be more for short qanats, i.e. up to 3/1000 for qanats up to say five kilometers, and less – down to 0.3/1000 in the case of longer qanats (Briant 2001: 157) .

20. Goblot (1979: 39) explains that *"the qanat pool could also serve the ice house in winter."*

21. In his interpretation of the Greek texts of Polybius, Briant (2001: 25) explained that the Achaemenid kings gave farmers the right of use for five generations of the land they irrigated. The comparison with Wulff – who said that tax concessions were granted for five generations - shows that there are variations in the interpretation of the old Greek texts of Polybius.

22. All photographs by the Author are contained in the Catalogue of Ice Houses and are available on request.

23. Indicated on the map by small streams.

24. Shown on the map as light areas.

25. The group numbers appear on the map.

26. For a complete soils description please consult Dewan and Famouri, *Soils of Iran*, 1964.

27. *Sâzmân-e-Mirâs Farhangi* (MF) means Cultural Heritage Organization.

28. Rutstein reported that this ice house was located about a mile from the center of Kerman (Rutstein, H., and J. Kroll 1980: 90). It is today completely encircled by the city.

29. Late in the work it became evident that this ice house had earlier been named Bibizeynab.

30. *Ganjnâmêh*, Cyclopedia of Iranian Islamic Architecture, consists of 20 volumes, of which Volume 17 deals with caravansaries.

31. The UK Institution of Structural Engineers issued a comprehensive damage report after the 2003 earthquake. (Motamed 2004).

32. See also Figs. 8.6 and 8.7 on pages 206-207.

33. See also Fig. 6.3.

34. Two alleys by the name of Ice House Alley (*koocheh yakhchâl*) were located in Isfahan; one at Ateshgah Street, and one in the quarter south of the Ferdowsi Bridge.

35. Such an ice house could have been similar to the thatched European models, cf. Fig. 1.1.

36. Page 96.

37. Ref. also Gye (1988: 129-144).

38. In the 5th millennium BC, modest structures at Sialk near today's Kashan were made of pisé (rammed earth), which in the 4th millennium was replaced by the newly invented mud brick; but at this period a brick was only a lump of earth, roughly fashioned between the palms of the hands and dried in the sun; hollows pressed into it by the thumb gave a key for the mortar joints. (Ghirshman 1965: 29)

39. The modern SI unit 1 MPa (megapascal) is equal to 100 t/m2.

40. In reference to General Dickson's experience during the Great War (1924: 165).

41. Marked © in the table in Fig. 7.14.

42. Locations refer to the list in Fig. 4.3.

Bibliography

Abbreviations

CAD: *Chicago Assyrian Dictionary*. Oriental Institute. Chicago: University of Chicago, Press, 1956-2011.

CHIr: *The Cambridge History of Iran*. Vol. 1: *The Land of Iran*. Edited by W.B. Fisher. Cambridge: Cambridge University Press, 1968.

DSDE: *Den Store Danske Encyklopædi*. Copenhagen: Gyldendal, 1994-2006.

EBr: *Encyclopaedia Britannica*. Chicago: Encyclopaedia Britannica, Inc., 1982.

EIr: *Encyclopaedia Iranica*. Center for Iranian Studies. New York: Columbia University, 1985-2011.

EI: *Encyclopaedia of Islam*. Leiden: Brill, 1954-2002.

EVA: *Encyclopedia of Vernacular Architecture of the World*. Edited by P. Oliver. Cambridge: Cambridge University Press, 1997.

GN: *Ganjnameh*: Cyclopedia of Iranian Islamic Architecture, Vol. 17. Edited by Kambiz Haji-Qassemi. Tehran: Shahid Beheshti University, 1996.

Alizadeh, S. et al
2002 *Iran: A Chronological History*. Tehran: Alizadeh Publishers.

Anaitallad, R. et al
1970 *Water and Water Works in Ancient Iran*. Tehran: Water and Power Ministry (in Farsi).

Badawy, A.
1966 *Architecture in Ancient Egypt and the Near East*. Cambridge, Mass.: MIT Press.

Bahn, P.
1996 *Archaeology: A Very Short Introduction*. Oxford: Oxford University Press.

Baker, P.

2005   *Iran. The Bradt Travel Guide.* 2nd ed. Bradt Travel Guides.

Bakhtiar, A., and M. Azad

2004   *Iran: The Cradle of Civilization.* Tehran: Gooya House of Arts and Culture.

Beaumont, P., G.H. Blake, and J.M. Wagstaff

1988   *The Middle East: A Geographical Study.* 2nd ed. London: David Fulton Publishers.

Beazley, E.

1977   "Some Vernacular Buildings of the Iranian Plateau." *Iran* 15: 89-102.

Beazley, E., and M. Harverson

1982   *Living with the Desert: Working Buildings of the Iranian Plateau.* Warminster: Arisand Phillips Ltd.

Beny, R.

1975   *Persia: Bridge of Turquoise.* Toronto: McClelland and Stewart Ltd.

Boisen, I.

1946   *Banen skal bygges på seks Aar* Copenhagen: Nyt Nordisk Forlag Arnold Busck.

Bonine, M.

1982   "From Qanat to Kort. Traditional Irrigation Terminology and Practice in Central Iran." *Iran* 20: 145-160.

Briant, P.

2001   *Irrigation et drainage dans l'Antiquité, qanats et canalisations souterraines en Iran, en Égypte et en Grèce.* Paris: Thotm Éditions.

Briant, P.

2002   *From Cyrus to Alexander: A History of the Persian Empire.* Winona Lake, IN: Eisenbrauns.

Browne, E.G.

1893   *A year amongst the Persians.* London: A&C Black Ltd.

Burke, A., and M. Elliott

2008   *Iran.* 5th ed. Lonely Planet Guide Book. Melbourne.

Buxbaum, T.

2008   *Icehouses.* Princes Risborough: Shire Publications Ltd.

Chardin, J.

1927   *Travels in Persia. 1673-1677.* Introduction by Sir Percy Sykes. London: The Argonaut Press.

Christensen, P.

1993   *The Decline of Iranshahr.* Copenhagen: Museum Tus-
            culanum.

Clark, K.N., and P. Paylore (eds.)

1980   *Desert Housing: Balancing experience and technology for
            dwelling in hot arid zones.* Tucson: University of Ari-
            zona, Office of Arid Land Studies.

Dabaieh, M.

2009   "Conservation of vernacular architecture as an inspir-
            ing quality: theoretical and practical study of Balat
            Village in Dakhla oasis." Universitas 21 International
            Graduate Research Conference: Sustainable Cities for
            the Future, Melbourne and Brisbane Nov 29-Dec 5.
            2009. http://www.universitas212.bham.ac.uk/GRC/
            GRC2009/Dabaieh.pdf

Dewan, M.L., and J. Famouri

1964   *The Soils of Iran.* FAO, Rome.

Dickson, W.E.R.

1924   *East Persia: a backwater of the great war.* London: E.
            Arnold & Co.

Dieulafoy, J.

1887   *La Perse, la Chaldée et la Susiane.* Paris: Hachette et
            cie.

Farshad, A., and J.A. Zinck

1998   "Traditional Agriculture in Semiarid Western Iran.
            A Case Study of the Hamadan Region." 16th World
            Congress of Soil Science Proceedings: Man versus
            Soil, 20-26 August, Montpellier. http://natres.psu.
            ac.th/Link/SoilCongress/bdd/symp45/118-t.pdf.

Fasa'i, M. S.

1996   *The Kavir Safari.* Tehran: Negar Books.

Fazeli, H., M. Salimi, and R. Young

2009   "Landlord Villages of the Tehran Plain, Iran, and His-
            torical Archaeology of Iran." *Iran* 47: 149-163.

Ferrier, R.W.

1996   *A Journey to Persia. Jean Chardin's Portrait of a Seven-
            teenth-Century Empire.* London: I.B. Tauris.

Fisher, W.B.

1971   *The Middle East. A Physical, Social and Regional Geog-
            raphy.* 6th ed. London: Methuen & Co. Ltd.

Frye, R. N.

1968   *Persia.* London: Allen and Unwin.

Frye, R. N.

1976   *The Heritage of Persia.* 2nd ed. London: Cardinal.

Fryer, J.

1992   *A New Account of East India and Persia: being Nine Years Travels 1672-81.* Vol. III. New Delhi: Asian Educational Services (first printed in 1915, London).

Geer, R.M.

1935   "On the use of ice and snow for cooling drinks." *The Classical Weekly* 29, No. 8: 61-62.

Ghazbanpour, J.

2005.   *Bam.* Tehran: Tiss Publishers (in Farsi).

Ghirshman, R.

1965   *Iran: From the Earliest Times to the Islamic Conquest.* London: Penguin Books.

Ghobadian, V.

1998   *Climatic Analysis of Traditional Iranian Buildings.* Tehran: Tehran University (in Farsi).

Givoni, B.

1976   *Man, Climate, and Architecture.* 2nd ed. Elsevier Science Ltd.

Goblot, H.

1979   *Les qanats. Une technique d'acqisition de l'eau.* Paris: Mouton Éditeur.

Godard, A.

1965   *The Art of Iran.* London: George Allen and Unwin.

Goldschmidt, A.

1991   *A Concise History of the Middle East.* Boulder: Westview Press.

Gye, D.H.

1988   "Arches and Domes in Iranian Islamic Buildings: An Engineer's Perspective." *Iran* 26: 129-144.

Herbert, T.

1928   *Travels in Persia 1627-29.* Edited by Sir William Foster. London: Routledge.

Hillenbrand, R.

1994   *Islamic Architecture: Form, Function, and Meaning.* New York: Columbia University Press.

Horne, L.

1994   *Village Spaces. Settlement and Society in Northeastern Iran.* Washington, D.C.: Smithsonian Institution Press.

Hourcade, B.

1994   "Les glacières du plateau iranien." *Luqman* X: 87-98.

James, P., and N. Thorpe

1994   *Ancient Inventions.* London: Michael O'Mara Books Ltd.

Kashraian, N.

2002   *Iranian Architecture.* Tehran: Agah Publishing House (in Farsi).

Keddie, N.R., and Y. Richard

2006   *Modern Iran: Roots and Results of Revolution.* Rev. ed. New Haven, Conn.: Yale University Press.

Lambton, A.K.S.

1953   *Landlord and Peasant in Persia: A Study of Land Tenure and Land Revenue Administration.* London: Oxford University Press.

Larsen, M.T.

1997   *Gudens skygge - det assyriske imperiums historie.* Copenhagen: Gyldendal.

Leick, G.

1988   *A Dictionary of Ancient Near Eastern Architecture.* London: Routledge.

Loveday, H., B. Wannell, and C. Baumer

2005   *Iran: Persia: Ancient and Modern.* 3rd ed. New York: Odyssey Publications.

Lovell, A. (Transl.)

1971   *The Travels of Monsieur de Thevènot into the Levant.* Originally published in 1687. London: Gregg.

Lundbaek, M.

1970   *Ishuse. Om isning, opbevaring og brug af is i ældre tid, især paa danske herregaarde.* Copenhagen: Institut for Europæisk Folkelivsforskning.

Makizadeh, M.

2004   "Ice Houses. The Art of Desert Architecture." *Farhang-e-Yazd* 5, Nos. 16 & 1: 41-47 (in Farsi).

Matheson, S. A.

1972   *Persia: An Archaeological Guide.* London: Faber and Faber Ltd.

Mathiasen, H.F., and E. Reitzel

1999   *Grundtræk af bærende konstruktioner i arkitekturen.* Copenhagen: Kunstakademiets Arkitektskoles Forlag.

Michell, G. (ed.)

1978   *Architecture of the Islamic World. Its History and Social Meaning.* London: Thames and Hudson.

Miras Farhangi (Iran Cultural Heritage Organization)

1999   *Ancient Water Buildings in Semnan Province.* Tehran: Ministry of Energy (in Farsi).

Modarres, A.

2006   *Modernizing Yazd: selective historical memory and the fate of vernacular architecture.* Costa Mesa: Mazda Publishers.

Motamed, J.

2004   *The Bam Earthquake of 26 December 2003, Iran.* London: Institution of Structural Engineers.

Motamedi, M.

2002   *Historical Geography of Tehran.* Tehran: Historical Geography Center.

Nicolaisen, Å. (ed.)

1978   *Lademanns Have- og Planteleksikon.* Vol. 15. Copenhagen: Lademanns Forlag.

Nielsen, A.K.

1935   *Marco Polos Rejser.* Copenhagen: Gyldendal.

Nippa, A.

1991   *Haus und Familie in arabischen Länder: Vom Mittalalter bis zur Gegenwart.* Munich: C.H. Beck.

The Oxford University English Dictionary

1967   Oxford: Oxford University Press.

Pazooki, N., and A. Shadmehr

2005   *Iranian Artifacts Registered in the List of National Monuments.* Tehran: Iranian Cultural Heritage Organization (in Farsi?).

Pope, A.U.

1965   *Persian Architecture: the triumph of form and color.* New York: George Braziller.

Porter, Y., and A. Thevenart

2003   *Palaces and Gardens of Persia.* Paris: Flammarion.

Pütt, K.

2005   *Zelte, Kuppeln und Hallenhäuser: Wohnen und Bauen im Ländlichen Syrien.* Petersberg: Michael Imhof Verlag.

Rahimi-Laridjani, F.

1988   *Die Entwicklung der Bewässerungslandwirtschaft im Iran bis in sasanidisch-frühislamische Zeit.* Wiesbaden: Dr. Ludwig Reichert Verlag.

Rainer, R.

1977   *Anonymes Bauen im Iran.* Graz: Akademische Druck- u. Verlagsanstalt.

Rugoff, M.

1961   *The Travels of Marco Polo.* New York: The New American Library.

Rutstein, H., and J. Kroll

1980   *In the Footsteps of Marco Polo: a twentieth century odyssey.* New York: Viking Press.

Sartipipour, M.

2006   *Knowledge Management of Rural Vernacular Architecture.* Tehran: Shahid Beheshti University.

Siroux, M.

1949   *Caravansérails d'Iran et petites construction routières.* Cairo: Institut francais d'Archéologie orientale.

Siroux, M.

1971   *Anciennes voies et monuments routiers de la region d'Ispahân.* Cairo: Institut francais d'Archéologie orientale.

Skibo, J.M., and M.B. Schiffer

2008   *People and Things: A Behavioral Approach to Material Culture.* New York: Springer.

Smith, A.

1966   *Blind White Fish in Persia.* London: Allen & Unwin.

Stevens, R.

1971   *The Land of the Great Sophy.* 2ⁿᵈ ed. London: Methuen & Co.

Strauss, M.J.

2005   "Old ways of water management spring up again in arid regions." *The New York Times*, August 20.

Tapper, R., and K. McLachlan (eds.)

2003   *Technology, Tradition and Survival: Aspects of Material Culture in the Middle East and Central Asia.* Portland, OR: Frank Cass Publishers.

Trinkaus, K.M.

1985   "Settlement of Highlands and Lowlands in Early Islamic Damghan." *Iran* 23: 129-141.

Troels-Lund, T.
1969   *Daglig Liv i Norden.* Vol. 3. Copenhagen: Gyldendal.

Tucci, G. (ed.)
1977   *La Citta' Bruciata del Deserto Salato.* Venice: Errizo Editrice.

Vahman, F., and C.V. Pedersen
1998   *Persisk-Dansk Ordbog.* Copenhagen: Gyldendal.

Watson, P.J.
1979   *Archaeological Ethnography in Western Iran.* Tucson: University of Arizona Press.

Wikander, Ö. (ed.)
2002   *Handbook of Ancient Water Technology.* Leiden: Brill.

Wilber, D.N.
1958   *Iran: Past and Present.* 4th ed. Princeton, N.J.: Princeton University Press.

Wills, C.J.
1891   *In the Land of the Lion and Sun; or, Modern Persia: Being Experiences of Life in Persia from 1866 to 1881.* London: Ward.

Wulff, H.E.
1967   *The Traditional Crafts of Persia, Their Development, Technology, and Influence on Eastern and Western Civilizations.* Cambridge, Mass.: M.I.T. Press.

Wulff, H.E.
1968   "The Qanats of Iran." *Scientific American* 218: 94-105.

Zanger, H.
2004   "'Anonymes Bauen' in Lehm- und Ziegeltechnik. Reiseeindrücke aus dem Iran." *Ziegelindustrie International* 11: 10-18

Zargar, A.
2006   *An Introduction to the Iranian Rural Architecture.* Tehran: Shahid Beheshti University (in Farsi).

MAPS

Atlas of Iran

1971. Tehran: Geographic & Drafting Institute.

Geological Map of Iran

1957. Tehran: NIOC.

Iran Geomorphology. Scale 1:2,500,000

1995. Tehran: National Geographic Organization.

Iran og Turan. Scale 1:6,000,000

c. 1925. Copenhagen: Koppels Forlag.

Map of Central Deserts. Scale 1:2,500,000

1992. Tehran: National Geographic Organization.

Relief Map of Iran. Scale 1:2,000,000

2005. Tehran: National Geographic Organization.

Road Atlas of Iran. Scale 1:1,000,000

2005. Tehran: Gitashenasi.

Satellite Map of Iran. Scale 1: 2,000,000

2004. Tehran: National Geographic Organization.

Soil Map of Iran. Scale 2,500,000

1961. Rome: FAO.

Soil Potentiality Map of Iran

1963. Rome: FAO.

The Cartographic Satellite Atlas of the World

1997. Worldsat International Inc.

The Middle East "A". Scale 1:4,000,000

1989. London: John Bartholomew & Sons.

Topographical Map of Iran. Scale 1:1,600,000

2006. Tehran: Gitashenasi.

Index

(YC means Yakhchal/Ice House)